STRATEGY

PART 1

Learn the skills used by the leading management consulting firms, such as McKinsey, BCG et al.

1ST EDITION

By Kris Safarova

STRATEGYTRAINING.COM & FIRMSCONSULTING.COM

We believe in the power of logic, reason, and a compelling narrative to teach our clients to solve mankind's toughest problems.

STRATEGY

Learn the skills used by the leading management consulting firms, such as McKinsey, BCG et al.

© 2021 Firmsconsulting LLC

A Kris Safarova | StrategyTraining.com & FIRMSconsulting.com Original

January 2021

Published & Printed in the United States of America by Firmsconsulting LLC, Los Angeles.

www.firmsconsulting.com

Firmsconsulting is a registered trademark of Firmsconsulting LLC.

Firmsconsulting business books are available at special discounts for bulk purchases for sales promotions or corporate use. Special editions, including personalized covers, excerpts of existing books, or books with corporate logos can be created in large quantities for special needs. For more information please contact **info@firmsconsulting.com**.

All Rights Reserved. This book or parts thereof may not be reproduced in any form, stored in any retrieval system, or transmitted in any form by any means—electronic, mechanical, photocopy, recording, or otherwise—without permission of the publisher, except as provided by United States of America copyright law. For permission requests, write to the publisher, at the address below

FIRMSCONSULTING L.L.C.
187 E. Warm Springs Rd.
Suite B158
Las Vegas, NV 89119
info@firmsconsulting.com

Disclaimer: This work contains general information only and is not intended to be construed as rendering accounting, business, financial investment, legal, tax, or other professional advice and/or services. This work is not a substitute for such professional advice and services, nor should it be used as a basis for any decision or action that may affect your business and/or career. The author and publisher disclaim any liability, loss, or risk that is incurred as a consequence of the use and applications of any of the contents of this work.

Terms of Use: This is a copyrighted work, and Firmsconsulting LLC companies ("Firmsconsulting") and its licensors reserve all rights in and to the work. Use of this work is subject to these terms. Except as permitted and the right to store and retrieve one copy of the work, you may not reproduce, modify, create derivative works based upon, transmit, distribute, disseminate, sell, publish, or sublicense the work or any part thereof without Firmsconsulting's prior consent. You may use the work for your own noncommercial and personal use. Any other use of the work is strictly prohibited. Your right to use the work may be terminated if you fail to comply with these terms.

Firmsconsulting and its licensors make no warranties as to the accuracy, adequacy, or completeness of the work or results to be obtained from using the work, including any information that can be accessed through the work through hyperlink or otherwise, and expressly disclaim any warranty, expressed or implied, including but not limited to implied warranties of merchantability or fitness for a particular purpose. Under no circumstances shall Firmsconsulting and/or its licensors be liable for any indirect, incidental, special, punitive, consequential, or similar damages that result from the use of or inability to use the work, even if any of them have been advised of the possibility of such damages.

ISBN 978-1-7340327-9-6

THIS BOOK IS DEDICATED TO MY FAMILY.
MAY THERE BE MORE PEOPLE LIKE THEM
IN THE WORLD.

IT IS ALSO DEDICATED TO OUR CLIENTS
AROUND THE WORLD WHO WORK HARD
TO SOLVE MANKIND'S TOUGHEST PROBLEMS.

WOULD YOU LIKE TO VIEW
EXCLUSIVE PREVIEW EPISODES
FROM THE PROGRAMS
ON THE PREVIOUS PAGE?

———

Visit

Firmsconsulting.com/promo

to submit your email.

You will be emailed the content at no charge

———

All content by
ex-McKinsey, BCG et al. partners.

CONTENTS

INTRODUCTION	15
ENGAGEMENT BACKGROUND	23
LATIN AMERICA BANK (LAB) REQUEST FOR PROPOSAL (RFP)	27
DESIGN THIS STRATEGY ENGAGEMENT	33
WEEK 0: PLANNING	37
1. Building up to the engagement.	39
2. Great strategy consultants can come from any background.	44
3. Why does Latin America Bank exist?	51
4. Should the state ever enter a market that can be served by the private sector?	57
5. Does LAB compete on risk or price?	62
6. Has LAB considered less risky ways to extract profits from the US market?	68
7. What is LAB's role relative to all other state entities?	77
8. Why relying too heavily on your McKinsey/BCG/Bain past employment is a trap.	82
9. Boutique firms need to be less aggressive but have intellectual firepower.	88
10. The quality of training is directly proportional to the impact of the engagement.	100
11. A good engagement structure assumes the client's preferred option is not valid.	107

STRATEGY

12. Basic logic can generate an 80%-accurate answer before detailed analysis is required. — 118
13. Ensure that the CEO smooths the path for the consultants. — 123
14. Forgetting the expectations exchange is probably the single biggest career killer. — 139
15. Most hard skills are a commodity in management consulting. — 145
16. Small signals on an engagement snowball into setting the tone. — 151
17. Partners expect efficiency and selflessness when communicating. — 157
18. Focus interviews are the heart of top-down analyses and must be done first. — 162
19. Are you designing a case study about a company or an attribute? — 170
20. Does your value system exist as words or in everyday actions? — 174
21. Internal strategy units sometimes feel challenged by external consultants. — 179
22. Military strategy teaches much about competition strategy. — 185
23. Demonstrated competency is at the heart of the best consulting. — 191
24. Competition strategy is partially about forcing your competitors to waste resources on preempting an action you will not take. — 199
25. The cost of capital differential is a key arbiter of LAB's options. — 207

CONTENTS

26. Women should not be punished for their beauty. — 212
27. Lack of confidence forces poor choices in image management. — 216
28. Reading and interpreting exhibits is a crucial skill. — 222
29. Having a reliable inside source at the client is a valuable asset. — 230
30. The team is structured to start like a greyhound, slow down a little, and end on a high. — 236
31. Case studies add value if you are clear about their purpose. — 241
32. The engagement office should be a safe zone, closed off from the client. — 247
33. Consulting teams should be trained to manage engagements for times when things go wrong. — 253
34. Interns are future CEOs and should be treated as such. — 257
35. Good training must adjust as the mood and energy levels of the participants change. — 262
36. It is a good sign to be genuinely excited the day before a major engagement begins. — 271
37. The ability to leave your ego at the door will make you a great consultant. — 277
38. Forget everything a firm claims to be. They are who they hire and what they reward. — 283
39. The role of a partner is to make the client successful. — 290

STRATEGY

WEEK 1:   INTERVIEWS AND ANALYSES — 295

1. The first few days are critical to set the direction of the engagement and analyses. — 297
2. Basics, basics, basics. — 305
3. Focus interviews guide the team and help build credibility. — 310
4. Credit guarantees are quickly identified as a potentially larger problem. — 317
5. When communicating with a partner, think about how to help him or her, not yourself. — 322
6. LAB is in a dire financial situation, driven by the credit guarantees. — 329
7. If the credit guarantees are so lucrative for the partner private banks, why is the product not growing? — 337
8. Take time to constantly adjust and improve your plans. — 346
9. Finding mistakes is not the same as solving a problem. — 355
10. Having a big ego is the worst baggage for a consultant. — 360
11. You can mainly bond with a client over non professional topics. — 368
12. Always check the source material. — 372
13. Take the time to ensure that a critical insight is understood. — 379
14. Shadow studies reliably test the initial hypotheses. — 385
15. Strategy consultants should spend more time thinking and less time analyzing. — 390

CONTENTS

16. The halo effect impacts just about every engagement. — 393
17. Be clear about definitions in an engagement. — 400
18. The value of one insight is greater than the volume of insights. — 409
19. Presentations are successful thanks to the pre-presentation. — 418
20. It is best to wrap up focus interviews and shadow studies as early as possible. — 422

WEEK 2, PART 1: INTERVIEWS, STUDIES, MEETINGS — 427

1. Force the manager to step into the leadership role. — 429
2. Don't let the business case analyses begin unless the planning is crystal clear. — 439
3. Case studies are hard work, requiring extensive corroboration. — 447
4. Learn how to get things done with low confidence. — 452
5. If LAB will be immensely profitable in twenty years, we would have failed. — 460
6. Commitment is more important than intellect. — 465
7. The real action begins when the analyses are done. — 470
8. Nimisha used clever techniques to assume leadership. — 475
9. This engagement matters to the US, which manages several large state banks. — 480

EXHIBITS

EXHIBIT 1:	Day 1 priorities for the team	93
EXHIBIT 2:	Distilling the story for the client	94
EXHIBIT 3:	The day before a major client update	96
EXHIBIT 4:	Analyses approach	102
EXHIBIT 5:	Key engagement questions	108
EXHIBIT 6:	Engagement activity activities	109
EXHIBIT 7:	Engagement timelines	110
EXHIBIT 8:	Decision tree of options outside retail	111
EXHIBIT 9:	Market-entry logic	112
EXHIBIT 10:	Market-entry options	113
EXHIBIT 11:	Focus Interview	128
EXHIBIT 12:	New consultants must master four foundational skills	146
EXHIBIT 13:	Shadow study template	227
EXHIBIT 14:	Issue map for a single work stream	300
EXHIBIT 15:	Team weekly / daily update report	302
EXHIBIT 16:	No-negative-precedents communication strategy	313
EXHIBIT 17:	Shadow studies	352
EXHIBIT 18:	Engagement progress	357
EXHIBIT 19:	Shadow study: the regional manager	410
EXHIBIT 20:	Shadow study: the branch manager's Tuesday activities	411
EXHIBIT 21:	Shadow study, branch manager's Monday activities	412
EXHIBIT 22:	Financial model architecture	444

INTRODUCTION

KRIS SAFAROVA, EDITOR
LOS ANGELES, 2020

tHE GOAL OF THIS BOOK is to help you think like a strategy partner and, more important, develop insights like a strategy partner.

Almost every management or strategy book is written after the fact. They are written years or months after the situation described. They are written after the authors have had time to sift through their extensive work and piece together a cohesive story. Hindsight is twenty-twenty.

Those types of books are valuable because they eliminate the noise; the authors sift out the dead ends they encountered, and the wasteful tasks and unproductive administrative nightmares they had to endure to, for example, obtain a key piece of data.

You will not see the numerous iterations before the authors arrived at their final framework. You will not know the piece of data, off-hand comment, article or client quote that sparked the evolution of the second, third, fourth and final iteration of the framework.

You will not see how the hypotheses evolve as vital information and clues are unearthed in conversations with the client, from analyses and team discussions.

You will not observe the choppy nature of how an insight develops. You will not see how an early version of an insight is discussed, dismissed, and sometimes forgotten until a key piece of new data makes it relevant again.

You will not see the numerous discussions to tweak and adjust hypotheses, insights, and the final messaging to the client.

What you get in those books is the final answer. You see the final framework that was developed. The final analyses. Neatly packaged and presented. You end up thinking strategy is a simple linear process where a few analyses offer an unambiguous answer.

This is the equivalent of reading President Dwight D. Eisenhower's biography to understand the mechanics of how to win a war and lead a nation to victory. You will understand the key principles, but you will not be able to go into battle. You will be ill-equipped to actually do the work. A military leader has to lead a unit to become a leader. They have to get their hands dirty. They need the experience. They need to make mistakes. They need to know how to recover from mistakes.

Those books provide valuable lessons and observations. Yet the experience is what shapes a leader.

This book is different and attempts to give you that experience. To see the messy steps involved. It was written in real time. The notes were written hours before an event happened or hours afterward, usually on the same day.

If you want to be a strategy consultant and be able to produce the analyses in this book, solve complex problems, and influence senior executives, we believe you need to know how messy it usually is.

There is rarely an objectively correct recommendation that stands out from all the options available to a client. It is very difficult to know if a strategy will work. A very good strategy often looks exactly like a very bad strategy. The results from a set of correctly structured analyses often tell us little by themselves.

INTRODUCTION

A new strategy for a client is about creating a new reality for a sector. We often don't know how competitors, suppliers, and customers will react. We have to predict those reactions when we offer a recommendation. That is certainly exciting. And it is a powerful skill to have.

But you need to know how many dead ends you will face and how we manage them, how much data is unused and how or why we decided to ignore this data, how we had to work with clients, how we collected data, and how we had to work with employees and stakeholders who oftentimes don't really want to help external advisors.

If you know that every consultant faces these problems, even those at the best firms, and understand how we navigate these problems, then you should feel better going in and not feel overwhelmed when you face such problems. You will not feel like a failure, and you will not feel that consulting is not for you.

Analysis is messy. Data is flawed. It has holes. Data is misleading. Best practices fail. Consultants uncover new information every single day of an engagement that slightly nudges the original hypotheses. The ability to remain flexible and adapt is what matters.

You will see that strategy is not a function of simply finding and plugging in a framework. Although there is a clear logic to the thought process. If you want to learn how to think like a strategy partner and create original solutions that solve complex problems, this book could be a good companion guide.

Strategy consulting is an art. There are core analytic approaches we use, but we encourage creativity when using them. We want to unveil this process. And we hope this book gives you an appreciation of how we do that work and the important role strategy consultants play in society.

The work we do changes lives. The work we do helps families, cities, regions, and entire countries thrive. What we do is important. You should be proud to be a strategy consultant, and you should always try to be the best strategy consultant that only you can be.

THE PROCESS

This book is based on the Market Strategy Entry Program[1] and the associated 270+ videos and 350+ analyses fully editable slides. The former is available to FIRMSconsulting Insiders and the latter is available to SLIDE members. The book is loosely inspired by a real engagement, though the name, identity and location of the client has been altered to protect the client's identity.

We asked the partner leading that engagement to document what transpired each day as he thought through the issues, managed the client, and led the engagement team on this complex assignment. We initially published those notes for our members on FIRMSconsulting.com

Those posts generated hundreds of comments. We have since reedited those posts into this companion book to accompany the online video engagement available to our Insiders. The study also inspired *Turquoise Eyes*[2], an educational novel.

We retained the chronological order of the posts because we wanted strategy consultants to see how things unfold over time. The goal is to show you how the partner arrives at the frameworks that will be used,

---

[1] https://www.strategytraining.com/market-entry-strategy-program

[2] Safarova, Kris, *Turquoise Eyes*, FIRMSconsulting, 2020, https://amzn.to/3bzVa6g

INTRODUCTION

how the team is managed in real time and how an insight is developed. We kept the tone of the partner's writing. Each ex-McKinsey, BCG, Bain et al., partner with whom we work brings his or her own distinctive style, humor, and wit. We did not want to change that.

SKILLS

This book, PowerPoint slides and the online video training program, as well as the book *Turquoise Eyes*, are complementary. The material in this book is different from what is covered in the videos. Most of the thinking in this book cannot be found in the videos or in *Turquoise Eyes*. In other words, this book is not a substitute for the online program and slides, and vice versa. Every slide prepared for the study can be found in the online program. They are often used separately but are best used together.

The videos and PowerPoints from the engagement contain the detailed analyses from the engagement and the training to work as a top-tier strategy consultant.

The book assumes the reader has some basic strategy, critical thinking, and problem-solving skills. Those are taught in our various online video programs, as well as in *The Strategy Journal*[3], and the *Succeeding as a Management Consultant*[4] books. Those books introduce the problem-solving process.

---

[3] Safarova, Kris, *The Strategy Journal*, FIRMSconsulting, 2020, https://amzn.to/2QGft9d

[4] Safarova, Kris. *Succeeding as a Management Consultant*. 2nd ed. FIRMSconsulting, 2020, https://amzn.to/3a3atTn

This book focuses on the journey the team will take to develop its insights. The insights rarely jump out of the analyses. The hard work to develop an insight begins before the analyses begin and once the analyses are done. Too much thinking about strategy assumes all that is needed is frameworks, hypotheses, and analyses, and the answer magically appears. Strategy is a process of constantly iterating the implications of the findings.

The book offers moments to pause and reflect on the personal skills the reader should be developing, and the best practices a consulting firm could follow.

THE TEAM

This engagement was unique in that many members of our community joined the engagement team in conducting the analyses. For example, when we needed to conduct focus interviews across the South, our community of readers went out and completed the focus interviews and collected photos on our behalf. More than one hundred of our readers participated.

When we wanted to document the process to apply for a small business loan, our community took on the task of visiting bank branches and documented the application process. All of this happened under our careful guidance, and all the information was fed back to the engagement team that led the engagement.

Our community followed the partner's notes and watched how we completed the entire engagement day-by-day and week-by-week. The engagement team itself was selected from our one-on-one coaching clients. We wanted to demonstrate that anyone could learn how to do insightful and influential strategy work under the right guidance. Even if one lacked a consulting background.

INTRODUCTION

Our goal was to show readers in boutique and smaller firms that anyone can do great work. Nothing stops you from doing deeply influential thinking. You don't need to work at one of the best firms to be one of the best strategists in the world. You don't need permission to solve complex problems.

An effective strategy advisor has a strong set of professional values upon which the analytical skills are assembled. That is the foundation of outstanding management consulting.

IS THIS FIELD FOR YOU?

In reading this book, you will effectively think through a complex set of issues to determine if the fictional Latin America Bank (LAB), a wholesale bank, should enter the very profitable US retail banking sector. Any thorough training program must be set in a region, cover a sector, and solve a functional problem, as this one does. LAB's quest is a hypothetical case, inspired by reality, that a team of strategy consultants study over eight weeks; the team develops analyses, hypotheses, recommendations and ultimately detailed proposals for LAB. The team has also developed a relationship with LAB executives that augurs well for work with the bank in the future. There are fundamental lessons at play in this case that should resonate with neophyte and seasoned strategy consultants alike.

Don't assume this book is not helpful if you are uninterested in banking, market entry or the US market. You will quickly find this book has little to do with market-entry analysis but rather it tries to answer the question the client should be asking but is not asking.

Any book that goes into sufficient detail will have to focus on a sector. The principles are all directly relevant to you, no matter where you work. Just adopt the process in your thinking.

STRATEGY

We need to go into the details to teach you how to make judgment calls and interpret the data. The LAB case is set in the United States' retail banking sector, and it tackles a strategy problem related to market entry. That said, we teach from first principles, so the training is relevant to anyone trying to learn how partners at McKinsey & Company, Boston Consulting Group, Bain & Company, and other strategy firms think.

ENGAGEMENT BACKGROUND

**A Hypothetical Strategy Engagement:
Understand the Quest of Latin America Bank (LAB)**

What would you advise LAB to do?

*Before the engagement begins:
Receive the assignment. Lay the groundwork.*

YOUR CLIENT, Latin America Bank (LAB), is a majority state-owned wholesale-only bank originally created to fund low-income entrepreneurs through four channels:

1. Development Financial Intermediaries (DFIs): DFIs are typically family-owned, single-branch lenders borrowing money from LAB to offer loans to mainly low-income immigrant borrowers in the border states of both the US and Mexico.

    There are eighteen DFIs offering loans from $150 million to $15 million. Eleven are large and seven are micro DFIs, offering smaller loan sizes of around $50. A few DFIs have up to twenty branches. Many DFIs are unprofitable and have collapsed. This is one of LAB's primary lending channels.

2. Equity grants: LAB sometimes takes equity stakes to fund entrepreneurs. This is a small part of the business. LAB works through the DFI and other channels to do so.

STRATEGY

3. Credit guarantees: Retail banks offer loans to low-income borrowers. LAB guarantees up to 80% of the face value of the loan's principal.

4. Mentoring and micro DFIs: LAB uses numerous other small channels, such as micro DFIs. Like the equity grants, this is a very small part of the business. Mentoring is a fragmented support service encouraged by LAB but not yet funded by LAB.

LAB has no branch network and no direct interaction with borrowers. It only works through retail distributors by offering funding for loans, taking equity positions, or guaranteeing loans where private retail banks may use their own funds.

LAB's focus on the US market is driven by banking legislation forcing them to be sustainable and competitive. Mexico's Former President Enrique Peña Nieto on Thursday, January 9, 2014, signed into law a banking sector overhaul designed to increase lending and boost growth in Latin America's second biggest economy.[5]

The legislation is among a series of major structural reforms that Former President Peña Nieto has pushed through Mexico's congress since taking office back in December 2012.

President Peña Nieto's primary focus is dismantling subsidies for bloated state-owned banks and enterprises. LAB is being forced into the US market to subsidize losses in its Mexican operations. Although it ignored the legislation for a long time, LAB is now being forced to act due to pressure from the government.

---

[5] "As the Mexican economy takes offer, new President Enrique Peña Nieto has a shot at redemption," *Independent*, http://blogs.independent.co.uk/2012/12/03/as-the-mexican-economy-takes-off-new-president-enrique-pena-nieto-has-a-shot-at-redemption/

LAB is incurring losses in Mexico since that is partially the role of a state bank—to provide needed services to the population, even at a loss, when the private sector is unwilling to step in.

> "From 2014, Mexico will count on a financial system that, in addition to being more solid and robust, will turn responsible lending into a growth engine."[6]

The legislation is, partially, trying to get state banks to distribute as much of their balance sheets into the market as possible. Yet, at least for LAB, most of the loans and credit guarantees offered in Mexico are taken across the border to start businesses in the US.

Close to 80% of the guaranteed money is taken across the border by borrowers or sent by borrowers to their families in the United States, where they believe the returns will be higher.

Many DFIs have branches on both sides of the border, allowing customers to continue the relationship once they move across.

The credit guarantees are not a focus of the engagement, since LAB believes they are a "high performing" business.

LAB is disappointed with the DFIs' performance and wants to replace them with its own retail structure in the US for these reasons:

> LAB is under pressure to lend more of its balance sheet.

> It believes the US market is more stable, larger, and more profitable given that is where most of its low-income indirect borrowers end up.

> LAB believes the DFIs are a bottleneck, poorly managed, and inefficient.

---

[6] "Mexico's president signs new banking reforms into law," Agence France-Presse, http://www.rawstory.com/rs/2014/01/mexicos-president-signs-new-banking-reforms-into-law/

LAB's internal strategy unit has made a strong case to build a US retail branch network, and the bank has already begun planning its market entry.

When issuing the RFP (Request for Proposal) and Terms of Reference (next page), LAB had already decided to enter the US market and was seeking an operations plan to do so.

The LAB RFP was specifically looking at how to set up a retail branch network using this process:

The RFP was issued on the assumption that the US retail lending (DFI) market was attractive to LAB, and that assumption should not be challenged.

The focus of the RFP was identifying the structure of an efficient retail branch.

A pilot design for the first branch was expected as the deliverable from the RFP.

All other LAB products and channels, such as credit guarantees, were outside the scope of the engagement.

A wide variety of firms, including McKinsey, BCG, and Bain, among others were invited to submit proposals for the engagement.

LATIN AMERICA BANK (LAB) REQUEST FOR PROPOSAL (RFP)

TERMS of Reference for Conducting and Producing a Feasibility Report That Will Demonstrate the Business Case for the LAB Retailing Plan

1. Type of Notice: Open Invitation to Tender

2. Contracting Division: LAB - Executive Office

3. Contact Person: The Internal Technical Advisor - Executive Office

4. Latin America Bank

    Latin America Bank (LAB) is an agency of the Secretariat of Trade and Credit of the Mexican government. LAB is a wholesale finance institution providing development finance to develop financial intermediaries (DFIs) for lending to small, medium, and micro enterprises (SMMEs).

    LAB also provides wholesale funding to large enterprises seeking funding via retail banks.

5. Nature of the Investigation and Project Scope

STRATEGY

The purpose of this investigation is to scope and design a comprehensive feasibility report that must be presented in the form of a detailed Pilot Retailing Implementation Program Plan that will be fed into and incorporated into the Corporate Business Plan of LAB.

The Plan must comprehensively expostulate all the implications to LAB in respect of extending its mandate to include Retailing as an additional SME financing option. The implementation will initially be on a pilot project basis. The Implementation Plan must contain the following detailed information as outlined below:

Pilot Retailing Implementation Plan Outline

1. Introduction
2. Scope of Pilot Engagement
3. Strategic Objectives
4. Target Market
5. Strategic Competitive Positioning
6. Operations or Lending Strategy Requirements
    a. Lending methodology
    b. Lending policies and procedures
    c. Lending criteria
    d. Lending service charter
    e. Workflow design
    f. Application forms (electronic and manual)
    g. Loan Committee submission format

7. Financial System Requirements
    a. MIS hardware and software requirements
    b. Policies and procedures
    c. Administration and control requirements
    d. Accounting requirements
    e. Reporting requirements
8. Human Resource System Requirements
    a. Staffing requirements
    b. Ideal organization structure
    c. Policies and procedures adaptation
    d. Staff training requirements
    e. Employment contract requirements
    f. Job grading requirements
    g. Remuneration strategies
9. Marketing Strategy Requirements
    a. Product offering
    b. Price positioning and strategy policy
    c. Promotional strategy, including sales and new business strategy
    d. Brand personality or image of brand
    e. Logo
    f. Brochures

STRATEGY

10. Pilot Project Office Location(s)
    a. Office location(s)
    b. Office specifications
    c. Office equipment requirements
    d. Office furniture requirements
    e. Office modification requirements
    f. Signage requirements
12. Key stakeholder consultation strategy
13. Detailed Pilot Project with Costing and Budget
14. Implementation Plan with Time Frames
15. Projected Financial Statements
16. Detailing a profile of a similar institution (in a peer country) elsewhere in the world
17. A detailed work plan must be provided in the submission outlining what will be completed on a biweekly basis, as well as the specific timeframes for the entire project, as stipulated below.

6. Expertise Required

The assignment calls for practical expertise preferably in preparation of SMME retail financing business plans or expertise in the banking industry.

7. Expected Outputs and Timeframes

The successful service provider must provide the final bound report covering items 1–17 in the outline stated above by May 30,

20TK, with the first draft submitted by May 20, 20TK. A detailed work plan must be provided in the submission outlining what will be completed on a biweekly basis. A monthly draft report document must be submitted to the contact person indicating the progress made. The successful service provider must be available for biweekly meetings with the contact person.

8. Assessment Committee:

   The short-listed service providers will be required to do a presentation to an Assessment Committee consisting of three Executive Committee (EXCO) members.

9. Assessment Criteria: The successful service provider will be selected on the basis of the following criteria.

   - Tender document presented.
   - Demonstration of previous experience or insights into some of the following: banking operations, SME financing, and compiling similar feasibility studies and plans.
   - Financial services product and product development knowledge.
   - Cohesion, complementarity, and diversity of skills as pertaining to the project.
   - Relevance and demonstrated understanding of the assignment during the presentation if short-listed.
   - Tenderers must demonstrate commitment to ethnic minority advancement.

10. Deadline for receipt of tender proposals: February 21, 20TK

11. Tender approved by: Managing Director

12. Tenders: All tenders must be submitted in sealed envelopes and addressed to the Company Secretary, LAB [Address redacted]. NB: Please note that tender proposals and quotations must be submitted in separate envelopes clearly marked as stated above.

DESIGN THIS STRATEGY ENGAGEMENT

BASED on the client brief and RFP, take some time to design this engagement. Answer these questions:

- What would be your problem statement for this engagement?
- How would you structure the engagement and staff your team?
- Over how many weeks would you run the engagement, and what would be the milestones each week and the major streams of work?

If you need some help, *The Strategy Journal*[7] provides a road map to break down the problem into issues, hypotheses, analyses, and work plans for a consulting team.

Once you are done, compare your design to the approach presented in this book and note the differences, such as:

- Why is there a difference?
- What assumptions did you make about the engagement?
- What lessons can you learn?
- What can you improve about your thinking and approach on Monday morning at 8 a.m.?

You may want to bookmark these pages and refer back to them often to see how your thinking differs from the actual engagement.

---

[7] Safarova, Kris, *The Strategy Journal*, FIRMSconsulting, 2020, https://amzn.to/2QGft9d

STRATEGY

DESIGN THIS STRATEGY ENGAGEMENT

WEEK 0

1 day

ONBOARDING THE INTERNS.

PLANNING AND STRUCTURING THE STUDY.

BUILDING HYPOTHESES, ANALYSES, A TIMELINE, AND A STORYBOARD.

LESSONS FROM A SENIOR PARTNER.

week 0:
PLANNING

The Senior Partner's Essential Observations on the Team, the Engagement, and LAB

---

1. BUILDING UP TO THE ENGAGEMENT.

Basically, we have a sleeping giant of a bank, a behemoth, which has developed specialized skills in managing risk when funding small entrepreneurs in Latin America. The bank has funded many Hispanics who take the money across the border into the United States and started small businesses. They also have a large base of clients in Mexico and other Latin countries.

The bank believes there is a large, profitable, and untapped market to provide micro, small and medium-size loans to entrepreneurs who are pursuing generally not-so-attractive businesses in the US.

The bank believes they can make this move work and have largely begun the implementation planning with their own internal strategy team. The internal strategy unit at the client, staffed by former consultants from McKinsey and BCG, are leading this effort.

We have been brought in by the CEO to see if the US market is, indeed, attractive to LAB.

With just 20-plus days to go before the engagement begins, we have a lot to do.

It will be interesting and challenging to determine if this banking client can build a business off rising US income inequality.

The problem with serving entrepreneurs at the bottom of the economic pyramid is that most microlending typically offers no path to the middle class. So, entrepreneurs earn some income and are slightly better off, but what happens next? Being marginally better off was not intended to be the American dream.

Yet the opportunity could be meaningful if we consider that close to 50 million Americans earn a yearly salary that is less than the minimum wage threshold. Very few entrepreneurs from this group would qualify for banking loans or any other financing to pursue an entrepreneurial path.

The bank believes offering a full-service banking product and finely tailored services via an accessible retail structure can change this, and they can profitably serve the low end of the market and provide entrepreneurial financing to this segment.

CAN THEY?

As the partner leading this engagement, I must heed the competing stakeholders at the bank who will all try to push their own agendas, which could include:

1. The retail banking operations staff will want the market entry to go ahead since it widens their empire.

2. The bank's internal strategy team will likely want to control the engagement and make the outcome support their existing conclusions.

3. The CEO may have an agenda we are yet to discover.

All the stakeholders will pursue their own agenda by latching onto some key issue impacting the client and presenting their approach as a solution to addressing this key issue.

The team thinks through the broad issues facing the company. This is the essence of corporate strategy.

Why is what's happening, happening and what would happen if we changed the outcome? We have identified thirteen considerations to keep in mind.

PAUSE & REFLECT

> What do you think are the most important issues to keep in mind for this engagement?

> Is this a market-entry strategy engagement?

> What other type of strategy engagement could this be?

> Why is it important to determine, from the beginning, the type of engagement?

WEEK 0: PLANNING

2. GREAT STRATEGY CONSULTANTS CAN COME FROM ANY BACKGROUND.

Your alma mater plays a minor role in determining whether you will be an outstanding strategy consultant.

1 NON-IVY MANAGER MBA + 2 IVY MBA ASSOCIATES

One of the most important roles a partner has is not to just help the company be successful, but to help the executives be successful in their careers. Guillermo, the client EVP assigned to work alongside me on the engagement, has very good qualities, and I can see him making a very big impact at the bank. We had a fairly long discussion this morning (yes, on a Sunday), and we discussed his career.

I will put together a plan to guide him through the process and make sure the findings don't surprise him. He should be able to seamlessly take over once we depart. Moreover, I will equip him to be a better executive at the bank.

In other words, one of my goals is to figure out how to make the banking engagement a success for both the bank and Guillermo.

I suspect my relationship still has to develop with the CEO before I can find ways to help him in his personal career. There is still time for that.

Let us introduce the fine team of interns selected for this engagement.

Engagement Manager: Nimisha B., an MBA student from a top-twenty program in the United States. Background in consumer-packaged goods and insurance before going on to enroll for her graduate studies. She holds an undergraduate degree in statistics and accounting. Nimisha is the youngest member of the team and fluent in English & Hindi. In a nutshell:

1. Nimisha demonstrated exceptional poise and communication skills during her case interviews. She was also very skilled at solving cases without using frameworks, wherein she relied on natural logic.

2. Nimisha finished her undergraduate degree with a 4.0 equivalent GPA from an emerging markets school. She may not finish in the top 10% in her MBA class. There is still a year, though, for her to turn that around.

3. Nimisha's hidden talent is singing Bollywood songs.

Associate: Peter Z. An MBA student at a top-three US program. He has a background in investment banking and private equity. Peter is the oldest member of the team and wants to return to investment banking or join a consulting firm. Peter is fluent in English, Spanish, and German. More about him:

1. Peter graduated with 3.8 GPA from an Ivy League school and has an impressive background in sports. He also has a natural skill in cases and was exceptional in communication. Peter will likely earn highest distinctions when he graduates with his MBA.

2. Peter's hidden talent is…We don't know yet. But we do know he is well-rounded with many interests, talents, and skills.

Associate: Albert G. An MBA student from a top-three US program. Albert worked in financial services equity trading before taking time off to support various social causes in Latin America. He founded a nonprofit and a start-up before enrolling in his MBA program. Albert is fluent in English and Spanish. More about him:

1. Albert graduated with a 4.0 GPA from an Ivy League school. There, he was captain of the rugby team and a tutor in the bridging program where he was voted "Teacher of the Year" two times in succession.

2. Albert's hidden talent is teaching Americans rugby over just one beer.

WHO IS A STAR MANAGER?

I have noticed that everyone who views the profiles of the team automatically asks an indirect question about why Nimisha was selected as the engagement manager. Guillermo asked the question pretty directly since he saw more of a finance background in the two associates on the engagement.

I suspect her non-Ivy background bothers others far more than it registers with her. I am not even sure she is aware of it—as it should be.

I had to remind him that we are relying less on past knowledge and more on the problem-solving process and on Nimisha's background in consumer-packaged goods, which would be useful.

Even so, we received a few emails from readers about why Nimisha was selected as the best person on the team and as the engagement manager.

Readers, and mostly tier-2 consultants, just assume that being the engagement manager means you are the best person on the engagement.

That is a significant misunderstanding.

If I had known each person on the team for two years and worked with him or her over that time, then yes, that assumption is correct.

WEEK 0: PLANNING

However, when I have an internship view of the candidates, then that assumption is no longer true. I have only known them for about two weeks before they arrived.

I would not make the most gifted team member the engagement manager.

That is Albert.

I do not want him to be bogged down by the daily burden of coordinating the team.

Albert needs to have freedom to roam around the engagement, under my guidance, and develop insights on the value analyses.

Nimisha is confident and a good coordinator; coupled with her intellect, she can manage the team.

That is a Sir Alex Ferguson lesson. Your best playmaker should not be burdened with the captaincy. They should have the freedom to roam around, knowing the captain will orchestrate the game around them.

Many assumed Nimisha was the best due to being assigned engagement manager. She is the best engagement manager, but I believe Albert will have the biggest impact.

When we split up for focus interviews, Nimisha will lead one group and I will be paired with Albert to guide him. No point having the partner and engagement manager in the same group. If this happened, who would make decisions in the other group?

Most of my lessons in business and leadership come from business, sports and the military.

Over the course of the next twelve weeks—two weeks before the engagement and ten weeks during the engagement—I will continuously stress a consistent message to the team.

STRATEGY

You can do many things in life: Play the piano, play football, go surfing, learn to code, etc.

What you do does not matter. How you do it matters, and it matters intensely. One person can make a difference. In fact, throughout history it has only ever been one person at a time that has made a difference.

I want the team to understand this. This is not an internship. That is just a title and a meaningless one at that.

We have the chance to change lives. If we do this right, people will look back and say our team led this, and the engagement made a difference. It made America a better nation and changed the lives of countless people.

It found a way to help immigrant parents and low-income earners find a new path to the American dream.

What could be a greater cause worth pursuing? I can think of nothing more important.

Consulting is an enormous privilege, and in ten weeks, who knows how much change we can affect.

We routinely ask our teams to summarize the final findings into a two-page report. A simple summary. Yet we sign that report.

Artists must sign their work. You must have pride in what you do. You must want your name to be attached to the engagement.

WEEK 0: PLANNING

PAUSE & REFLECT

> Do you think generating pride and excitement in a team's work can radically change the quality of the output?

> How will you know when you are ready to manage a business analyst or engagement team?

> How are you actively tracking the skills needed to be a manager and/or partner?

> How do you balance taking ownership of your development versus relying on your mentor to develop you?

STRATEGY

3. WHY DOES LATIN AMERICA BANK EXIST?

The founding mandate of an organization plays a critical role in determining its strategy to execute that mandate.

LAB'S MANDATE

The first consideration is important but largely ignored.

What is the bank's mandate? Why was it created? And, obviously, how does entering the US market help the bank fulfil its mandate?

The bank received money from a national government, and the government is the majority shareholder. What does the government want from their investment and from the bank?

Is this expectation explicitly captured in the bank's founding articles of incorporation or a national law that governs the client? They are a quasi-state-owned bank working with large private-sector equity investors. Which investor's needs take precedence?

Ultimately, the success of the bank is determined by its ability to meet the written expectations set out during its founding. We need to be vigilant about this and ensure that anything that takes them away from this goal is not pursued.

A cursory reading of the banking founding legislation indicates the client is governed by a legislative mandate, which requires them to:

1. Earn a return greater than or at least equal to inflation.
2. Increase employment in the country.
3. Increase job creation.

No matter where we go with the analyses, we need to be guided by the mandate of the bank. We obviously need to validate this by getting a copy of the original articles of incorporation and the bill that went through the senate.

A simple reading of the situation would say entering the US market does not help the bank create jobs in its own market so it should not do it.

Unfortunately, the situation is not that simple. That brings us to consideration two: cross subsidization.

CROSS SUBSIDIZATION

There are two ways to look at this. One is **option A:**

A. Is Latin America Bank (LAB) so unprofitable in its current business and/or markets that it wants to enter a foreign country and charge higher fees to generate higher returns and bring this money back to Latin America to cover losses?

This is not implausible. If LAB needs to create jobs in Latin America and this critical need is forcing the bank to incur losses, it will need to offset this somehow.

Otherwise, the bank would need government funding in perpetuity to offset the losses from entering markets with low to negative returns. The Industrial Development Corporation (IDC) did this in Mozambique when they funded smelter operations, by requiring higher returns than they could get in their home market.

Yet the IDC issue was slightly different, which brings us to **option B:**

B. Is the client, Latin America Bank (LAB), profitable in its current business and/or markets but unable to extract higher returns due to its social mandate like job creation? Does it, therefore, want to enter a foreign country and charge higher fees to generate higher returns and bring this money back to Latin America to do more good work?

Again, this is a very plausible option.

But there is a wrinkle.

If a Mexican national, for example, crosses the border to work in the US and remains a Mexican national, should LAB charge him or her higher interest rates for a loan merely because he or she is based in the US?

Is that ethical? Is it legal?

They are separate issues.

What about Mexicans who borrow money and create businesses in Mexico? Are they treated differently?

This is definitely an area the team needs to consider, and these are some of the tough decisions we need to make. Yet the answer is fairly simple. Interest rates are set by legal jurisdictions, so the legal statues for interest rates where the loan is approved will apply.

It is worth remembering the Emma Lazarus quote etched into the tablet on the Statue of Liberty .

> "Give me your tired, your poor,
> Your huddled masses yearning to breathe free,
> The wretched refuse of your teeming shore,
> Send these, the homeless, tempest-tost to me,
> I lift my lamp beside the golden door!"

My final note is an important reminder. Since we personally want this banking client to succeed, we need to take the opposing stance and play devil's advocate.

We need to prove this will not work. If we are wrong, everyone is happy. If we are right, we saved the bank's capital.

Bias is no friend to a consultant. We need to be right, irrespective of our personal preferences.

PAUSE & REFLECT

> Why do you think LAB is entering the US market?

> Due to issue A or B above?

> Does the option you selected change your proposed engagement structure?

> Does LAB want to enter the US market or is it being forced to show it is trying something to improve?

STRATEGY

4. SHOULD THE STATE EVER ENTER A MARKET THAT CAN BE SERVED BY THE PRIVATE SECTOR?

Economics teaches us that the state should not undertake work that the private sector could do better.

WHY NOW?

We continue the off-site planning for the engagement, thinking through the broad strategy issues and considerations that box in the bank's options. There are about two weeks before the team goes on-site to begin this landmark engagement.

We will keep these issues at the back of our mind as we go out and structure the analyses, particularly the focus interviews.

The third issue relates to the timing. Why does the bank want to do this right now?

    a. Is there an unsaid reason that is compelling the bank now to go after one of the world's most competitive financial services markets? Most likely.

    b. Does the bank have weaknesses in its core business forcing it to make this shift? Maybe, but unlikely.

    c. Is the bank in danger of running out of cash and does it want to reinvent itself? Unlikely.

We will only know more once we start, but this area is outside our scope. We just need to consider the implications by showing the bank how much the US banking venture will cost before it creates positive free cash flow or how much it will consistently lose.

STRATEGY

WHAT IS THE ROLE OF A STATE-OWNED BANK?

And now, the fourth issue. The fourth and second issues are somewhat related.

The second issue asked the question: What is the role of this bank? The role will be determined by the act of government that incorporated the bank, or shareholder agreements, whichever may be the case.

The fourth issue, meanwhile, sits above that and looks at the role of a state-owned bank, any state-owned bank for that matter. What should its role be?

State banks typically exist to invest in areas of the country that need investment but generate such a low return that private banks would not go near those areas. There is just no meaningful return. Therefore, the role of the government, and by extension a state-owned entity, is to make investments that the country needs, but that the private sector is, for whatever reason, unable or unwilling to make. So:

1. Should the state bank invest in sectors/regions that are attractive financially, since those attractive sectors and regions would likely receive private sector funding anyway?

2. In essence, should LAB compete with the private sector, or should they pursue different return ranges?

The second issue provides part of the answer. Possibly.

If the bank is going after the US market to secure higher returns to invest in parts of Latin America with low to negative returns, then it could make sense.

Yet how sustainable is this cross-subsidization model?

Does it mean LAB is a bank with good and bad assets? How does it manage these assets? Does it ring-fence them?

What are the implications of raising capital against bad assets?

Again, this is outside our scope, but our work will inform the bank of the implications.

PAUSE & REFLECT

> Do you agree with the economics view that the state should not compete with the private sector?

> What are the implications for LAB if you accept this view?

> Would your proposed engagement structure change if you did not accept this view?

> When should the state compete with the private sector?

WEEK 0: PLANNING

5. DOES LAB COMPETE ON RISK OR PRICE?

A bank can only compete on one of these levers.

RISK VS. PRICE

It is crucial to understand LAB's age and particularly the age of its debt book.

When LAB was conceived, it would have been capitalized with billions of dollars from the government and/or any outside partner investors. Remember, the client is a state bank.

At first, LAB has on its balance sheet all this capital, which it borrowed at relatively low rates since there is a belief in the market that the bank is backed by the government. True or not, this is what the market thinks, even in the US where Fannie Mae and Freddie Mac are assumed to have government backing and will not be allowed to go bankrupt.

Those low rates are LAB's key competitive advantage. It can compete against some private banks by offering clients lower interest rates on loans because its cost of capital was lower due to the implied government guarantee.

Over time, as the bank increased loans to the market, two things happened.

> First, if the bank is staying within its mandate of serving those with very low income and a higher risk profile, its bad loan book increases. It is hard to avoid this.
>
> Second, as the bad loan book increases while the market continues lending money to LAB at lower rates, the difference

between LAB rates and that of private banks becomes smaller and smaller, since LAB's risk increases with the size of its bad book.

Why do we care about this?

LAB, like any other state bank, will be able to wield this interest rate differential as a younger bank. As it gets older, its ability to do this diminishes, for the reasons listed above, and it needs to find new ways to compete.

So, we need to carefully analyze its loan book, and bad loan book, to see if it can continue competing on pricing. And if so, by how much, and if not, how else can it compete?

Logic would dictate that if LAB honored its mandate of helping those with poor credit scores and access to the market, its bad loan book would increase.

The question is, how bad is the bad loan book?

WHY THE UNITED STATES?

The US is a massive market. Everyone wants to be there, and everyone wants to have dominant market share. Issue 6 considers why LAB wants to enter the US market specifically.

In essence, the bank will build a retail-banking network, and those networks need scale to pay off the high fixed-cost investment.

Yet the issue is more nuanced than this.

LAB wants to generate a certain return from financing small businesses in the US, primarily among immigrants. So, it needs to deploy capital in the form of loans, equity investments, credit guarantees, and more.

From the profit, it needs to pay off its retail structure investment and then move the remaining profits back to the head office.

If LAB is going after such a large market as the United States, it must have a lot of capital to both fund the investment and create a loan book. Why does it have so much undeployed capital that needs to find such a large parking lot?

It implies LABs current markets suffer from a lack of absorptive capacity. That means the markets it now operates within cannot absorb the cash LAB wants to lend. In basic terms, there are not enough viable opportunities to fund.

So, what is it about the US market that makes LAB think there is a greater absorptive capacity? A larger market does not correlate with a larger absorptive capacity. Many barriers, such as legislation, interest, and competition, can reduce the absorptive capacity.

WHAT ANSWER DOES THE CLIENT WANT?

The seventh issue relates to the client's bias. The client is already preparing for implementation.

The internal strategy unit contains several alums: a roster of ex-McKinsey, ex-BCG, and ex-Bain principals, managers, associates, and analysts. Several of the EVPs running key divisions are also ex-partners.

The internal strategy unit believes entering the US is a good idea, and the people there have done some studies to support this.

In fact, the CEO initially discussed focusing the engagement on a plan to make the implementation work. Our view was that we needed to make sure the economics make sense before proceeding. We have seen numerous such ventures fail and simply relying on detailed studies done by outside parties was not an appetizing idea.

Aggregating the detailed studies from external parties does not lead to a better engagement. It leads to a summary of errors.

The only reason we were successful in being awarded the role of serving the client is because of this focus on testing the idea more rigorously. The board would want to see that it makes sense, and I have rarely seen a board use the findings of an internal strategy unit for these big decisions.

There are just too many conflicts of interest, as well as other issues that we will mention later.

STRATEGY

PAUSE & REFLECT

> Why is the client so intent on entering the US market?

> Should the client's high confidence in this idea imply we should find a way for them to execute this strategy?

> How would you use LAB's cost of capital as a strategy weapon?

WEEK 0: PLANNING

STRATEGY

6. HAS LAB CONSIDERED LESS RISKY WAYS TO EXTRACT PROFITS FROM THE US MARKET?

Physically entering a market is a means of last resort.

HAVE THE EASIER OPTIONS BEEN ELIMINATED?

The eighth consideration is one of the most important. At some point, probably around the second update, we would need to use this consideration to reframe the issues.

When considering market-entry cases, most consultants forget that no company or CEO wants to take on the hard work of entering a new country. It requires too much effort.

Most executives do not want to be a part of the vanguard arriving in a strange new country (all countries are strange to new arrivals) to set up offices, obtain licenses, hire staff, and build the necessary infrastructure. This is often not a fun experience. It can be demoralizing and depressing. Especially with the inevitable legal and other problems that would crop up, while your normal support system is not there.

What they actually want is exposure to the profits. Entering the market is one way of capturing the profits, but not the only way. With this in mind, you open a world of possibilities.

When a CEO elects to enter a market via mergers and/or acquisitions (M&A), he is implying that other forms of market entry, such as exporting intellectual capabilities including white labelling, licensing, outsourcing, and partnering have failed or were deemed less attractive.

LAB must only consider an acquisition or Greenfields direct market entry when easier forms of entry were carefully considered and decided against. Other forms of market entry could include:

1. LAB does white labeling: The bank produces financial products that are sold by the DFIs under the DFI brand to entrepreneurs.

2. LAB does another form of white labeling: The bank offers credit guarantees so that retail banks can offer loans to entrepreneurs. LAB will then cover a percentage of the loss incurred by the bank.

3. LAB licenses its capabilities: The bank could offer its credit scoring or other methodologies to a US bank interested in this market.

4. LAB becomes an outsourcee: LAB can become the back office for a US bank in many areas like claims processing, credit scoring, and more.

All four options allow LAB, or any company for that matter, to enter a market without directly entering a market.

We may not immediately realize it, but we are all familiar with these business models.

If you are on vacation in Aruba and walk into a shop to buy sunglasses, the odds are you will find sunglasses priced from $5 for everyday brands to hundreds of dollars for designer brands. I think it's fair to assume Louis Vuitton, Porsche, Burberry, Dolce & Gabbana, and many others do not have offices in Aruba.

They don't have offices in every market where they want to participate.

STRATEGY

What they will have is a licensing agreement with someone like EssilorLuxottica.

Each brand will agree to the conditions under which EssilorLuxottica can use their name to sell sunglasses. In this licensing agreement, each brand has found a way to extract the profits from the market without entering the market.

EssilorLuxottica has entered the market. Not the brand.

This is similar to the licensing agreements movie and TV studios sign with Netflix and Amazon Prime. A studio executive in Hollywood is probably not thinking how to enter the tiny country of Lesotho in Africa.

The market is just too small to warrant his attention and/or the cost to set up an office and strike licensing deals. Netflix solves this problem in one stroke. It is Netflix that enters the market. And the studio gets its profit from the market without entering the market.

Think of those branded but relatively cheap mobile phones sold by telecom networks like Sprint or Verizon.

Somewhere there's a company with the capability to make this phone; it used to be in Taiwan, but it's probably in China today and will likely be in India tomorrow. Lacking the money and resources to build a brand and retail operation in a foreign market, the company will white label the phone, meaning to manufacture it without the manufacturer's logo, but with the logo of the company selling the phone.

It's the same for many store-branded food and clothing products. The list can go on and on.

In outsourcing, a manufacturer in Taiwan may not be able to enter the US market to secure orders. So, it would outsource sales and distribution to another company in the US. Yet by bringing the manufacturing to Taiwan, it achieves the goal of generating profits from a new geography and avoids the costs and hassle of setting up a US operation.

We have to prove that white labeling, and other forms of market entry, are worse options than direct entry. Otherwise, why enter the market directly when a white labeling joint venture allows the bank to capture profits from the market, without incurring the risk of entering the market?

Many of LAB's decisions are governed by the expectations of its primary shareholder. We will be provided the following information to commence the engagement:

1. The act of government under which the Secretariat of Finance and Public Credit chartered the bank.

2. We will have access to LAB's audited financials going back five years, along with the auditor's unsealed notes. For each audited page of the financials, there are on average 3.4 pages of notes.

3. Audited financials of the DFIs.

4. Government projections on sector job creation in the US, Mexico, and three other Latin American countries.

We will only have access to them, though, when we arrive on-site in a few weeks.

WHAT IS THE COST OF CREATING A JOB?

This is the ninth consideration.

LAB is doing all of this to create jobs. That is the bank's mandate, which we will confirm via the acts of government.

How much does it cost them to create one job, and what is an acceptable amount?

If it costs $1,000 to create one job, is the return measured (Option 1) via the taxes the recipient provides to the government or (Option 2) via the trickle-down multiplier?

Option 1

In this option, for example, if taxes the borrower paid amount to $740 (for simplicity, assume this is a lifetime tax revenue from one new taxpayer), do we say the loan resulted in a loss of ($1,000 − ($1,000 − $740) − (cost of providing the loan))?

Option 2

If $740 in taxes was paid (for simplicity, assume this is a lifetime tax revenue from one new taxpayer), but the borrower spent $2,300 buying supplies, food, and material (for simplicity, assume those are purchases over the lifetime of this borrower) that created jobs in the economy, do we measure that multiplier effect?

This is a tough one. LAB wants to measure option 2, which will produce a higher number. And this is not even accounting for the impact on family members. If the borrower's children are better off, should that additional monetary contribution to the economy be taken into account? What about the borrower's grandchildren and other family members?

There is a problem with the trickle-down multiplier. It will create a bigger number but little of the additional money goes

> to LAB; a fraction of it goes to the government in the form of taxes.
>
> Therefore, LAB still ends up with a loss, despite the newly measured impact on the economy.
>
> Or is there an Option 3 where we measure LAB's profits after its cost of capital?

Does the government and LAB's investors want to accept this loss just to feel good about helping the economy?

What constitutes failure for LAB:

> Creating and sustaining many jobs at an accounting loss.
>
> Creating and sustaining many jobs at an economic loss (accounts for the cost of all inputs, including its cost of capital, and takes into account the opportunity cost).
>
> Significant profits while ignoring the segments it was meant to serve.
>
> There are other options we will discuss later.

Thinking about all the possible losses across the different segments and sectors make us believe that cross subsidization is a plausible initial hypothesis.

The only logical reason to enter the US will be to cross subsidize lower returns or losses in Latin America.

Job creation is not the prevailing mandate of the bank in the United States. Profits are.

Yet job creation is the prevailing mandate in Latin America.

That job creation costs money since LAB is trying to fulfill an institutional void. An institutional void means there is no system and infrastructure in place to provide these services, and therefore the costs to do so are usually much higher. If this infrastructure were in place, the private sector would probably enter and piggyback on it to serve the market.

In other words, Mexicans setting up businesses in the US actually benefit Mexico more than the US, provided Mexicans in the US are funded by LAB, which can move the profits south.

It is crucial to remember these differences in mandate between the US and Mexico as the engagement progresses.

Is this a modern take on remittances?

PAUSE & REFLECT

> How should we measure success for LAB overall?
> What is the right way to measure the costs and benefits of creating a job?
> What are the trade-offs in that method?

STRATEGY

7. WHAT IS LAB'S ROLE RELATIVE TO ALL OTHER STATE ENTITIES?

Latin America Bank has to play the position it was intended to play in the government's game plan.

LAB'S ROLE

We are more likely to find unhealthy and underperforming state-owned enterprises, given the reason why they were founded in the first place. After all, most SOEs were created to make investments that are either uneconomical or too risky to attract the private sector.

Therefore, poorly performing SOEs could very well be the norm at the beginning of their mandates. Their strategic importance to the rest of the country may be far more valuable than their profits.

In the tenth consideration, we need to look at LAB's evolution over time and the role it should be playing at this point in time. If it was created to initially serve a role at a loss, has it succeeded in laying the institutional infrastructure to attract the private sector?

And if not, why not? Does this mean LAB will operate at a loss?

In the eleventh consideration, we must think about LAB relative to the state-owned banks funding agriculture, roads, factories, houses, and more.

These banks work in concert. For example, in an impoverished town in Mexico, the infrastructure bank may seed the development of a new $1.1 billion processing plant. This investment alone will generate significant returns for the government and the bank.

Yet the workers need homes, sewage facilities, water, electricity, roads, food, and much more. Some of these initiatives will not be profitable. LAB may fund, at a loss, entrepreneurs setting up food trucks for the workers.

Yet the government accepts this because the net return from this investment cancels out all the losses and will still yield a significant profit. But if the homes are not built and the workers are not fed, the overall investment fails.

In this investment, LAB suffers a loss for the greater good. But are all its losses for the greater good? Is that its accepted role? Will it ever work alongside its sister banks and make a profit?

In fact, it may be in the interest of a country to have a portfolio of state-owned companies occupying different quadrants on an economic-profit curve going from losses to profits. This is the twelfth consideration.

As an SOE is created, it may underperform. Yet as the market matures and the SOE develops an effective business model, it could revive itself and start thriving. At this time, it may be ready for privatization.

The government could use the proceeds to create a new SOE addressing another critical gap in the market.

This cycle could continue so that the state is able to focus on different areas of development. South Africa did just this when the Industrial Development Corporation (IDC) funded Sasol. The success of Sasol produced generous dividends, which the IDC used in other investments. The privatization of Sasol eventually produced a windfall, which the IDC used to repeat its strategy.

Sasol continues to be a major investor in South Africa and a successful integrated energy and chemical company. Such an example shows what is possible with the appropriate strategy, state backing, and execution and a long-term mindset.

Care must be taken to avoid sweeping and inaccurate generalizations about SOEs. While many underperform and are unhealthy, there are many that clearly outperform their private-sector peers.

The latter group has become the envy of many and the benchmark against which their private-sector brethren are measured. As emerging markets grow and prosper, we expect to see many more such thriving SOEs emerge.

Finally, and this is the thirteenth consideration, the antidote to underperformance and poor business practices isn't necessarily privatization or even partial privatization.

In many cases, it is just not commercially feasible to fill a gap in the market and the privatized entity may well ignore its social commitment in pursuit of higher profits. That is, some markets are so unprofitable that no one can make money serving the market. Still, the citizens of that market need to be served.

This is an important point. If we go back to the issue of the government taking on roles that the private sector cannot or will not undertake, it's usually because the risk-adjusted profits are too low for the private sector.

In these cases, privatization will fail. That is because the private investors will turn the company away from meeting the unprofitable need the organization was originally intended to meet. This may very well be a need that has to be met for the country to develop and prosper.

The long-term solution is to ensure a high enough standard of living and low enough cost of doing business to encourage the private sector to invest and free up the government's capital commitments.

STRATEGY

PAUSE & REFLECT

> Would all strategy consultants assume a state-owned entity is a failure if it is unprofitable?

> How should a city, region, state or country manage its portfolio of assets to achieve sustainable and humane growth that benefits everyone?

> Is LAB a candidate for privatization?

WEEK 0: PLANNING

STRATEGY

8. WHY RELYING TOO HEAVILY ON YOUR MCKINSEY/BCG/BAIN PAST EMPLOYMENT IS A TRAP.

If your claim to fame is that you are ex-McKinsey, you will not build a firm to overtake McKinsey because you need McKinsey to be strong for you to have credibility.

COOL VS. RIGHT

I need to think how I will manage the engagement manager and how she will manage the team.

For obvious reasons, this is not a typical banking engagement. The team has little consulting experience, though some have interned at the best firms and will also have a full-time partner on the engagement. Senior partners like me are not assigned full-time to work on an engagement. Principals are—with support from partners.

Do I serve as the de-facto manager, or do I empower the engagement manager? What will be our plan for engaging the client?

Moreover, how do I balance the need to be hip and cool versus the need to be right?

With politicians, all justly focus on social issues like housing, banking, and access to services, and it is very popular to focus on these trendy topics.

The danger with trying to be trendy is that people, executives included, try to accommodate social trends without fully thinking through the implications.

We need to be sure that the bank's strategy to enter the US market is economically sound and the best plan for the bank. It may very well be a great opportunity but just not for this banking client. The last thing we want is the press celebrating the bank for its noble intentions when it may end up bankrupt in three to six years because the economics just did not work.

In some ways, we may end up being the only intellectually sober people at LAB. We need to let the economics speak for themselves, and if the economics are not great, offer suggestions on how to improve them.

If the economics cannot be improved, then sometimes a client needs to walk away from an opportunity.

Every market is financially viable. It may, however, not be viable for every company's cost structure and ability to maintain a competitive advantage.

Given the approach we are taking, which includes challenging the client's deepest beliefs, how does the client perceive us? Do we have the credibility to challenge the client?

THE PARITY TRAP

LAB employs many ex-consultants and maintains a very large internal strategy unit.

How would they perceive a team of ex-consultants, irrespective of their pedigree?

The reality is that, to them, we can only have parity to their skills. If they think that we think our prime value is that we are ex-consultants, then they will simply see us as being no better than they are.[8]

This is known as the parity trap. Once the parity trap snaps shut on us, you can expect the bank's employees to challenge us.

This is why so many ex-consultants try to specialize in a sector or area—to avoid the parity trap. Since the ex-consultant's seemingly greatest advantage is his or her previous employer on his or her resume, that person will have no apparent competitive advantage among other alums of his firm.

They try to build a new competitive advantage through specialization. That is why so many ex-McKinsey consultants end up specializing; with thousands of alumni prowling around for work, being just another alum is not enough.

In fact, why hire the ex-consultant when you can hire the firm?

The bottom line is that we will receive a frosty if not hostile reception, even from alums of the same firm. Many view the firm as strong, but they do not necessarily view alums of the same firm this way. After all, most people at McKinsey are managed out because they were not good enough to be promoted to the next level.

We will have to develop a plan to overcome the parity trap.

---

[8] https://hbr.org/2013/10/consulting-on-the-cusp-of-disruption

HOW MCKINSEY AVOIDS THE PARITY TRAP

When McKinsey arrives at a client's office and wants to present a recommendation, it may get challenged at times. But most of the time, it will be able to get away with anything. The same applies to BCG, Bain, and other top firms.

I am going to use a military analogy, but please do not treat your client as the enemy!

With McKinsey, in many ways, we see the firm's intellectual army. It shows you it's overwhelming intellectual superiority so that it will not be challenged by alums, publications, awards, or influence.

That is why these firms invest so much time in these things.

In military terms, this is called the Powell Doctrine. It means deploying such overwhelming resources to a situation that the enemy capitulates just by looking at what they are up against. The Powell Doctrine does not mean going to intellectual war, or any war for that matter. It means showing the opposing side that they should not even consider an attack.

What happens when you are a boutique firm of ex-consultants? If no one knows you well, how can they know the advantage you have? How can they know the army you have behind you?

It is a little like a schoolyard. You will be picked on until you show the bully you will not be picked on.

PAUSE & REFLECT

> Have you experienced a situation where a client challenges you since they perceive you to have a weaker background?

> How do you manage this?

> What would you do differently in the future and why?

> What would you do when your stellar credentials cannot impress a client?

WEEK 0: PLANNING

9. BOUTIQUE FIRMS NEED TO BE LESS AGGRESSIVE BUT HAVE INTELLECTUAL FIREPOWER.

The Ranatunga Doctrine implies moving so rapidly through deep insights that you leave competitors in your wake. The lesson: Do less but do it well.

THE LAZINESS OF EX-CONSULTANTS IS AN OPPORTUNITY

How do we overcome this problem at a boutique firm?

The parity trap is one where two alums of the best firm see themselves as being at parity. In other words, an ex-BCG partner leading a bank does not necessarily think another ex-BCG partner running his or her own boutique consulting firm is any better and will usually not hire that person for advice.

They would simply hire BCG.

Yet the parity trap has one flaw.

When consultants leave the best firms, many fervently believe they have earned their stripes, earned recognition, and should be rewarded for the time they have served at the firm.

This expectation is the problem. Most consultants, who join industry, are unwilling and sometimes unable to maintain the intensity required to keep their skills sharp, check their work as carefully and push through for the deeper findings. They focus on being accepted by their new peers.

In other words, they believe since they earned their stripes, they can get away with doing a little less by relying on their reputations.

This creates an opportunity. If you are an ex-consultant who can maintain the intensity required to develop deep insights and if you are willing to push the envelope just a little more, you will have a glorious career.

It is a small advantage, but it will make a huge difference.

That is how we will overcome the parity trap. By being willing to go just a little farther in checking, thinking, and assessing the issues.

If this is the strategy, what is the plan for engaging the client?

ENGAGING THE CLIENT

It's important not to become defensive when critiqued. It is better to offer to meet later and walk away until that meeting. Do not become emotional or ridicule the client—even in private.

Even if the client mentions a rival firm fifty times in a meeting, you should not mention this firm. Why advertise for them?

Knowing when to present and waiting for an opportunity to demonstrate the rigor with which we are approaching things is vital. It must only happen when the team is ready. That is why we do not meet the client for an update until we are ready.

That first impression may very well be our last impression.

The internal strategy group has already done many studies on entering the US market. Before going on-site, knowing that they are not going to check things as carefully (ex-consultants typically do not maintain the same vigor in their work), I can reasonably assume they are going to base their analyses on a lot of third-party documents.

For example, they will read books, articles and interviews about other banks that have done similar things.

Now, when we present our first update after the focus interviews (we usually start strategy studies with focus interviews), they will challenge us about something in that meeting. Ex-consultants tend to challenge. That is the single tool they can deploy to show they are paying attention. The same way they like to offer advice and suggestions to improve. They believe it is expected of them.

We can stop the attacks by explaining that we spoke to the source, the company itself, that we did not merely read the article about the company, and that, therefore, our findings are different. Of course, this has to be done in a delicate manner.

This simple exchange sends a direct signal to the internal consultants, and others, that we:

1. Are extremely thorough and, in fact, more rigorous than they have been.
2. Rely exclusively on primary data versus reported, third party information.
3. Have relationships they probably do not have.

This tactic usually stops the criticism.

Now you can see why the focus interviews are so important. It is crucial that our first update is based on facts, and facts cannot be challenged. Therefore, we cannot be challenged.

Once the unnecessary critiques stop, the engagement team must focus on continuing to build momentum.

How do we accomplish that?

THE RANATUNGA DOCTRINE

As I mentioned earlier, when I was in the firm as a partner, I followed the Powell Doctrine of managing clients and engagements. Because I could.

Boutiques will have to follow a different strategy because no matter how many types of alum staff our engagement, including former partners, it is assumed they will not have the expertise of McKinsey, Bain or BCG, and we will be constantly harassed for that.

There is a way to stop this from happening.

The Ranatunga Doctrine basically means that you blitz the client intellectually. Not in terms of volume, but in terms of the insights you generate, and you do that literally from the first day. And not just insights. Because to produce insights one needs the ability to manage organizationally and to structure the engagement to manage those insights and deliver those insights in a very professional way.

Note, "blitz" does not mean "be rude." It means being very articulate and having the ability to shift a discussion onto a logical argument when people stray from a discussion point, which they invariably do when they are emotional.

Most consultants who form boutiques try to first become friendly with the client, not alienate the client and then slowly grow into the role and show progress. Boutiques, of course, need the work to survive. And the client knows the boutique firm will agree to everything and anything because they need the work. The client will therefore have the leverage.

We are not going to do that. That is what the internal units and the internal strategy unit expect. We report to the CEO and our job is to get to the answer.

STRATEGY

By doing this, we shift the leverage to our side.

Where does the doctrine originate?

I grew up watching football and basketball, though my brothers liked cricket, which I felt was slow and boring. Who has five days to watch just one game, which could end in a draw anyway?

Eventually, the International Cricket Board set up one-day games that last just eight hours(!). Though, even that was very slow. The batsmen would take their time settling in and it only got exciting in the last few hours.

In the 1996 ICC World Cup, a little team called Sri Lanka captained by Arjuna Ranatunga, so chronically overweight that he needed to bring in a stand-in runner, and coached by Dav Whatmore, who only played eight games in his entire professional career, were the underdogs.

What could an overweight captain and a coach who had not played much actually do?

Plenty, due to the way they read the rules of the game.

They ended up deploying a completely different strategy that changed the game of cricket forever.

They realized that in the first fifteen overs, think of it as the first 30% of the game, the opposition could not place too many men on the edge of the very large playing field. In baseball terms, this means bringing all but two of your outfielders to stand just 5 to 10 meters away from the infield.

They exploited this.

They used two batsmen, Sanath Jayasuriya and Romesh Kaluwitharana, to smash the ball all over the field since there was no one to catch them at the edge of the field. Once they were done, they sent in solid closers like Aravinda da Silva to finish the job and drive up the score around the terrified outfielders.

WEEK 0: PLANNING

This changed the game completely.

Rather than starting slow and building up, they basically hit the accelerator from the start of the game.

This attacking style won them the World Cup and most teams now use this style.

The Ranatunga Doctrine will be our approach and I have used it many times before this situation. It works like this:

1. Ramp-up rapidly and keep that heavy pace right to the end. You can see this in **Exhibit 1**, which outlines that tough first day of the engagement where we want rough storyboards. This planning is also an indication of our focus.

   EXHIBIT 1: Day 1 priorities for the team

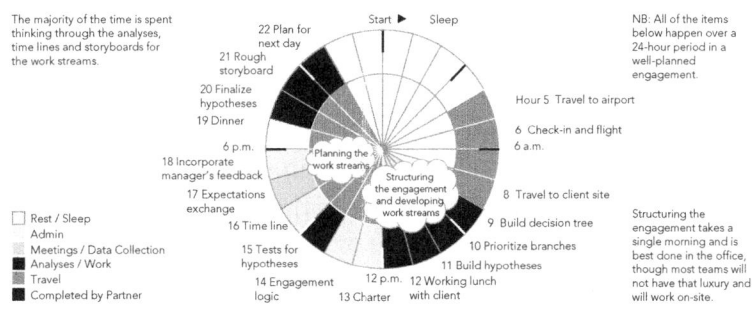

The central part is building a powerful and compelling message for the client. Why would LAB want to do anything unless it energizes the bank, solves its problems and creates a worthwhile risk-adjusted return that exceeded their cost of capital?

STRATEGY

They would not.

Therefore, an exciting part of the process is that day when the team gets together, **Exhibit 2**, to review all the work and generate the overall storyboard. Later we will break down this process into more steps.

EXHIBIT 2: Distilling the story for the client

Bringing the analyses together is a nerve-wracking process since it implies most of the work is already done

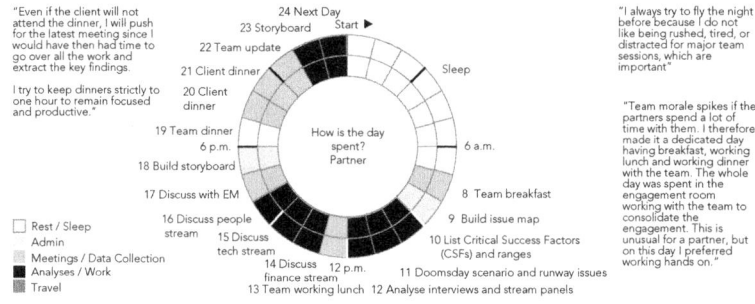

Later we will talk about pre-presents which imply the slides are done days before a major presentation. Even so, as you will notice from **Exhibit 3**, we run things tightly all the way into the first client update.

There is a lot of fun in all these steps. It's always important to remember that it's not money, titles or the client standing that will truly inspire a team. Consultants, even the client, wants to spend time with the senior partner.

They want to learn. They want to have deep and meaningful conversations. So, my plan is to spend a few hours in the evening with the whole team over pizza to help them with the work. This is what they want.

This will inspire them and it's at the core of the mentorship model. It's also a significant cost saver. The team will learn far more from observing a senior partner than they could ever learn from internal training sessions.

And some things are best taught in person. See how partners dress, act, speak, talk, carry themselves, handle questions, offer advice, etc. This is just as important as the analyses.

So, I am also doing this to have a better team. It's not philanthropy. It's simply a win-win situation. For the client executive updates, we keep the teams focused on just a few things, such as:

1. Have fun and be accountable while using the underlying problem-solving process and be creative.

2. Know the source material and legislation governing the client versus only reading the sound bites and quoting anecdotes.

3. Insights first, and we make friends only if doing so does not compromise our findings.

4. Less volume of work, but a focus on deep insights that must challenge the client's deepest assumptions. That is, very few slides are eventually presented.

5. Strip out the emotion and have economic / rational arguments to support all recommendations.

STRATEGY

EXHIBIT 3: The day before a major client update

The day before a major presentation is tough since the partner usually wants explanations and analyses

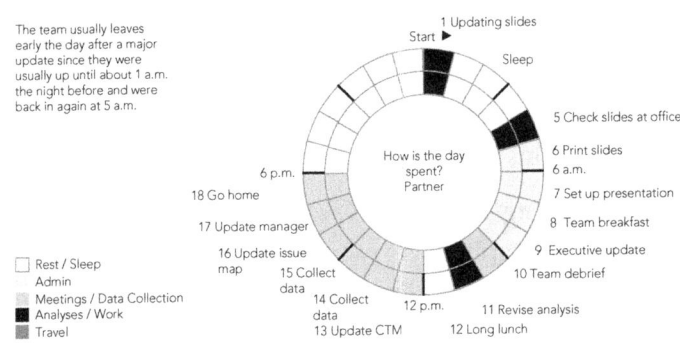

In this style, we will use the internal strategy unit's struggle to catch up, and since they are usually behind, they cannot legitimately co-opt the engagement if they cannot keep up with us. The CEO will also like it if we can produce deeper insights than he has.

The key here is stamina. It is very hard to work at this incredible pace. Burnout is common, so I need to ensure that the team is very focused on just the most important areas.

The Ranatunga Doctrine is not the same as the Powell Doctrine.

Maybe that is worth clarifying.

RANATUNGA VS. POWELL DOCTRINE

In the Powell Doctrine, you look so powerful and capable that no one will dare challenge you. So, you actually do not have to do much.

In the Ranatunga Doctrine, since you do not appear to look powerful, you have to pull the trigger, so to speak. You have to show people just how good you are.

If your confidence is built on the fact you went to Harvard, Stanford, Yale, or another Ivy League school, then you rely on the Powell Doctrine.

Your show of force, so to speak, is your education. You hope people don't challenge you due to the school you attended.

Consultants who use the Ranatunga Doctrine are highly prized since they rely on their demonstrated competency to gain respect. These types of consultants are incredibly impactful.

However, when it comes to building relationships with the most senior clients, no matter who you are, you need to be able to demonstrate your competency.

Clients typically expect a firm of ex-partners to focus more on the high-level executive issues. We are going to attack the problem from both sides: Understanding the contours of the issue and a rigorous understanding of economics.

PAUSE & REFLECT

› How do you manage situations when your credibility is challenged?

› What would you need to change in the way you work, train your mind, exercise, manage your personal life, etc., to employ the Ranatunga Doctrine?

› If you are unable to employ the Ranatunga Doctrine, what are your alternatives?

WEEK 0: PLANNING

10. THE QUALITY OF TRAINING IS DIRECTLY PROPORTIONAL TO THE IMPACT OF THE ENGAGEMENT.

Engagement teams should be supported by great training on engagements.

PRE-ENGAGEMENT ONBOARDING

As the interns prepare to arrive from their various MBA programs, I wanted to have regular conference calls to help them prepare and understand the culture, attitude and style of the way we approach problems.

Having so many updates before the interns start is uncommon, even at the best firms, so this is a luxury that I hope they will use to their benefit.

The agenda for this call is simple:

1. Provide the high-level engagement background.

2. Forget what they think is management consulting and focus on our guidance.

3. Ensure that they internalize the blistering pace at which we will work. It will astonish you, and them, to see what we will produce in the ten-week period. Again, the level of insights and not the volume is most important.

4. Explain the culture and value system we will use.

5. Get them comfortable asking for help, realizing that within the team they need to spend less time trying to look good and more time asking for help.

6. Emphasize the importance of taking initiative.

Unfortunately, I cannot provide more details to them until they arrive and sign the full nondisclosure agreement. If I want them to take away one thing, it is the pace at which we will need to work to understand the economics of this problem.

Far too much emotion and far too many anecdotes are being used to make massive decisions.

I will also send them a reminder about emailing me a list of their expectations from the internship and overall engagement.

I want them to look for second- and third-order expectations. In other words, they will need to make a list and ask themselves why they want these expectations to be met. Then they need to reword the expectations with their refined answers and repeat the process.

This forces them to get to the root cause of the expectation.

Then send it to me and I will discuss this with them when they arrive.

TOP-DOWN ANALYSES

LAB recommended we use an unbanked expert from the United States to work with us on the engagement. They believe he can add value, given that he understands the market well and worked on the initial studies LAB did internally.

This is not a bad idea. By working with him, we have someone they trust who, provided things go well and he understands our approach, findings, and research.

STRATEGY

The team will have to focus on three areas for the initial part of the top-down analyses, as shown in **Exhibit 4**. The case studies will begin now but will probably not make it into the first client executive update. Like the day-in-the-life-of studies (DILOs), the case studies will also provide benchmarks, such as:

1. Analyses of the bank's current financials to see how the bank is performing.

2. Focus interviews with a range of stakeholders, including government, banks, NGOs (nongovernmental organizations), LAB's partners in the US and local market intermediaries.

3. DILOs for the bank's agents working with borrowers in the field, clients of the bank (borrowers), and the intermediaries (distribution network) who help the bank find clients.

EXHIBIT 4: Analyses approach

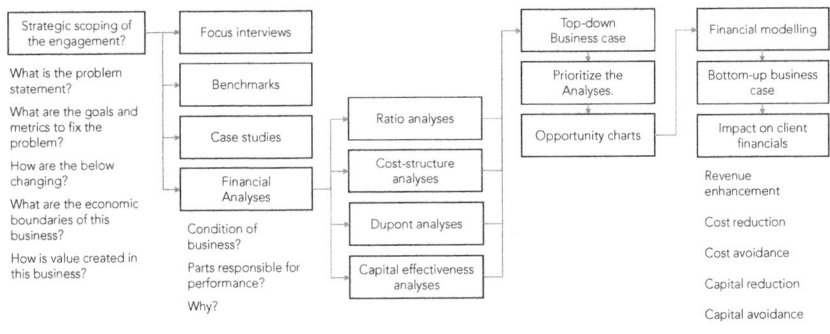

WEEK 0: PLANNING

Normally we would present the top-down financial analyses, a.k.a. "the size of the prize" in the first update. However, we will not do so here.

We will present a brief analysis of the financials earlier, but we will keep this for later updates. There are sufficient insights to be gleaned from the focus interviews and case studies alone.

I will spend the next few days thinking through how this works and whom we need to interview. In particular, the bank has intermediaries in the United States and Mexico to whom it provides financing, and these intermediaries find borrower clients. The bank also works with other banks in Mexico and Guatemala who have the same model.

We need to spend time understanding the economics of the intermediaries since this is what the bank would want to re-create if it entered the market directly with a retail structure. LAB intends to displace its current retail distribution network.

Would the intermediaries mind such an intrusion? Could the bank run the retail structure better?

Every time we present a finding, someone will say, "Have you looked at...."

Therefore, we will have to conduct our very own case studies to understand why some ventures were successful and others were not.

Since we are looking at micro, small, and medium-size businesses in the US, primarily in the South, we can consider a wide range of countries. The client has recommended Poland, Indonesia, Bolivia, the Dominican Republic, Kenya, Thailand, and, of course, the famous Grameen Bank of Bangladesh. Grameen and its founder, economist Muhammad Yunus, won the 2006 Nobel Prize for innovating microcredit, or life-changing small loans to poor individuals.

I would want to be very involved in the case studies to prevent them from becoming simple desktop research. We want to speak to the clients, managers, partners, and management of the agencies and companies we end up choosing for case studies.

We also want to review major failures—and there are plenty of those.

WEEK 0: PLANNING

PAUSE & REFLECT

> Why are values such an essential part of management consulting?

> Why do we have a top-down step in the study?

> What is the difference between financial analyses and financial modelling?

STRATEGY

11. A GOOD ENGAGEMENT STRUCTURE ASSUMES THE CLIENT'S PREFERRED OPTION IS NOT VALID.

Merely doing what a client wants will probably not make you a great consultant.

JOBS VS. PROFITS

What if...

> The sector with businesses that generate the highest returns for the bank
>
> ...is the smallest or shows a low growth rate
>
> ...and does not create many jobs?

This is something we need to reconcile in the engagement. Are we pursuing the most profitable sectors or those that create jobs? Is there a perfect balance?

Should the bank worry about job creation at all? Of course, the bank's mandate will guide us on this, but we are yet to see that document. Remember we are still in the planning stages before we arrive at the client's premises. It can only guide us, and there will be contradictions we would need to highlight and present a path around.

I suspect people will not worry much about this in the United States, but it will matter in Latin America.

Although we have a high-level approach to the engagement, which we used to secure the work via the written proposal, in the next few days, we will meet Guillermo to learn which areas the bank wants to prioritize.

We will thereafter adjust the engagement based on that discussion.

STRATEGY

We chose to ask the right questions for LAB (see **Exhibit 5**), and we did not assume entering the retail market in the US was the best option. Our process:

We will **first** determine if the channel can serve as a source of cross subsidies, given LAB's capabilities. In other words, can it be profitable and sufficiently profitable for LAB?

If so, **second,** we must determine if the US is the best market to serve as a source of cross subsidies for the loss-making domestic operations. Why not Brazil, Colombia, or Argentina?

If so, **third,** we must eliminate all other forms of market entry before recommending a direct market entry.

If so, **fourth,** we need to determine if the DFIs can be improved to fulfill LAB's mandate without LAB taking direct control.

Finally, we would need to determine if LAB should build a retail channel or acquire the existing DFIs.

EXHIBIT 5: Key engagement questions

The first step is to use the engagement structure/framework as a base to plan
ENGAGEMENT LOGIC, A.K.A. THE FRAMEWORK

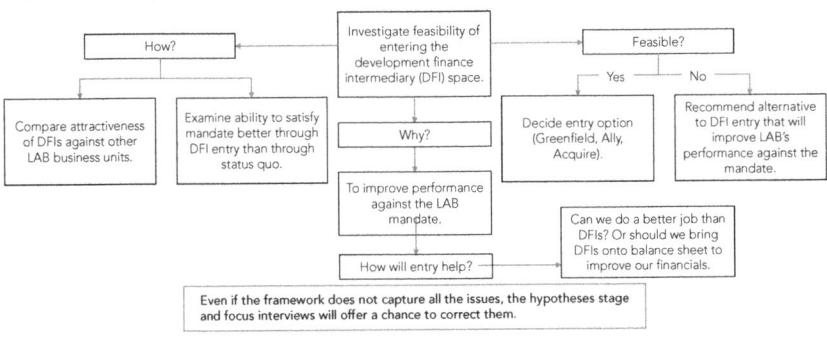

In **Exhibit 6**, we present a rough breakdown of the key activities the client can expect. This also helps the team understand how we will pull everything together.

In this breakdown, we presented an option where direct retail entry in the US would turn out to be the best option and set aside time to begin mapping out the pilot.

We are almost certain this will not be the case, and once we disprove the economics of directly owning the retail channel, the engagement will change considerably. We don't know what we will find and what the new priorities will be.

Yet, like all engagements, it will change.

EXHIBIT 6: Engagement activity activities

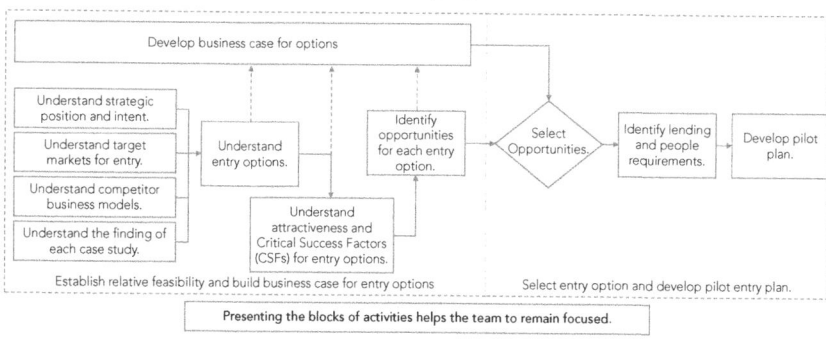

The rough timelines, in **Exhibit 7**, are also based on the assumption that we would proceed to the retail pilot. This is important to remember.

Even if we are certain it will change, we have to present what we think the client thinks will happen. This is why it's important not to assume an engagement structure is fixed when you review any letter of proposal or even the first update to the client.

Here, everything is presented as a traditional market-entry case. Yet this is not a market-entry case, and we will adapt this as we proceed. Sometimes, at least initially, it's easier to use the language a client is familiar with.

What we will find from our analysis will determine what we will prioritize in the study. And while we have some hypotheses, we are bound to find critical areas that may require more urgent attention.

EXHIBIT 7: Engagement timelines

The final step: convert "information needed" to "analyses needed," or simply add a timeline to the information
ENGAGEMENT ACTIVITY TIME LINE IN WEEKS BEGINNING:

June 16	June 23	June 30	July 7	July 14	July 28	Aug 5	Aug 12	Aug 26

- Understand key stakeholder requirements.
- Analyze entrepreneur microfinance market
  - Value chain, competitors, segments
  - International and local case studies
- Develop critical issues and hypotheses
- Understand business models and agree on entry options.
  - Agree on relative attractiveness of options.
  - Understand business models.
  - Define capability gaps.
- Agree on entry-option opportunities and prioritize.
- Determine lending, people and budget requirements
- Develop business case for options
- Determine pilot implementation requirements

Both options will work.

While the analysis considers the economics of the retail channel, we are also thinking through what will happen if very early on we discover the retail option to be invalid.

In **Exhibit 8** we present these options. It's important to remember that senior partners often have a long-standing relationship with a client. So, it's very rare we would be blindsided by a significant issue that we have not heard about before.

Yet it can happen, since every long-standing client starts with that first engagement. This is, hopefully, the case with LAB, and it is, therefore, possible we will find things we don't know because this is our first engagement for LAB.

EXHIBIT 8: Decision tree of options outside retail

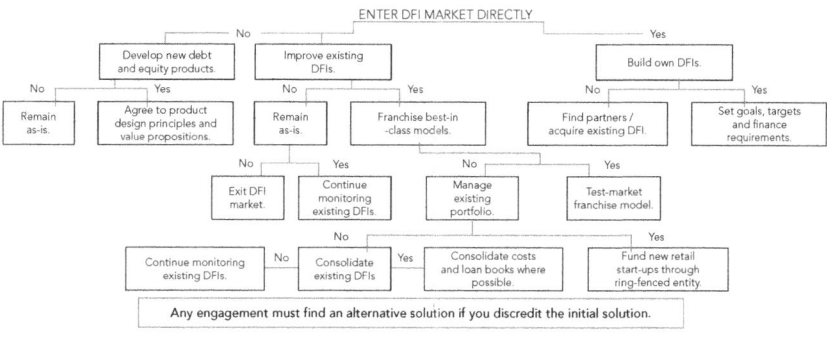

LAB's great challenge, as a wholesaler, is to distinguish between its clients, DFIs and other banks, and its recipients.

LAB has no direct connection to its recipients and must pick where in the value chain (**Exhibit 9**), it will operate and how it will do so to serve its recipients. It needs to find a way for both its clients and recipients to benefit.

STRATEGY

This can be difficult, but it's a fairly common approach. The same way a CGP/FMCG company works through a supermarket to serve consumers. The CGP/FMCG company must develop products and set pricing that encourages consumers to buy the product and customers (the supermarkets) to carry the product.

The main difference being the supermarket only wants customers who have money and can pay for the soup before they take possession. LAB, however, wants to target customers with very little money and ask the distributors to bear some of the risks of nonpayment.

EXHIBIT 9: Market-entry logic

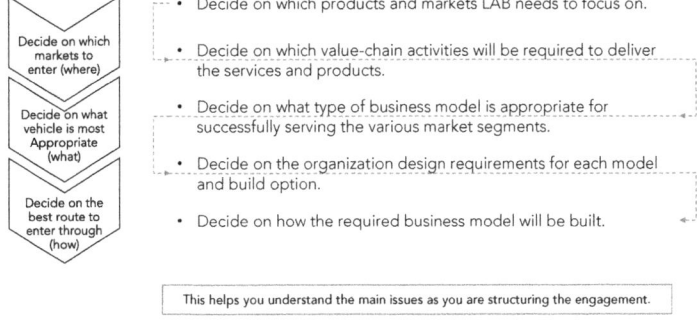

As part of being MECE (mutually exclusive collectively exhaustive), we present market entry on the far left for the client's benefit. See **Exhibit 10.**

However, our focus will be to keep LAB out of the retail market, assuming our hypotheses are correct, and find ways for them to work via distribution partners (on the right side of the exhibit).

Though the focus will shift to service level-agreement (SLA) management, LAB will need to become more of a hub to provide guidance, tools, best practices to its partners. Right now, LAB only provides some funding and a guarantee. It relies on the retail partners to use their own best practices.

EXHIBIT 10: Market-entry options

Explaining that entering the US market should be the option of absolute last resort stunned the bank's executives
LAB'S OPTIONS (EXPANDED)

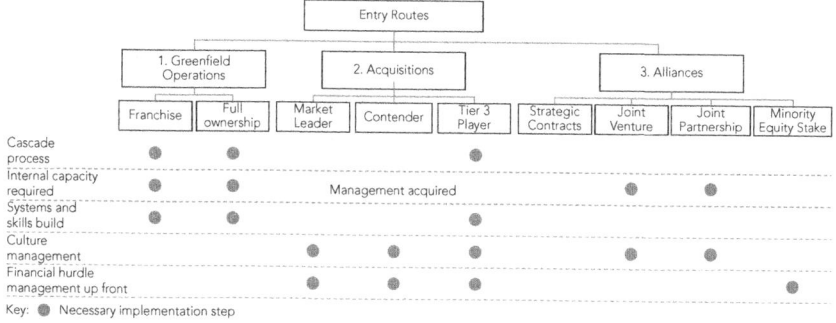

Most of this morning will require me, as the senior partner, taking a shot at structuring the focus of the engagement. I will do this mentally as I take a shower or have coffee. I will not need to sit at a desk to do this. Despite what LAB thinks, I do not believe setting up a massive retail structure is feasible.

We now need to prove that. It is only useful, if it can be proven. So, most of the early engagement will focus on the economics of the retail structure to provide entrepreneurial funding.

Whether we prove the structure viable, or not, the direction of the engagement changes dramatically. Options:

1. If the retail structure is viable, do we need to thereafter to focus on implementation?

2. If the retail structure is not viable within the US market, do we need to consider whether there is another way to enter the US market?

3. If the US market is not at all viable, irrespective of the entry mechanism—and we believe this is unlikely—is there another way for LAB to meet its mandate?

How will we calculate the demand for venture funding among the unbanked in the US?

As we think through the approach the team will need to take to work out the economics of the retail structure. This is a role normally reserved for the engagement manager and principal, but in this case, given the inexperience of the team, the partner must do it. We need to estimate demand for loans, and, so far, there has not be a good method presented anywhere.

We will likely need to find a way to break out demand by sector and sector size. We assume the economics of the retail micro business is very different from the economics of a medium- or small-size retail operation.

We see a lot of literature and studies using assumptions, benchmarks and guides from studies done in Mexico, Brazil, Bangladesh, and so on.

It is not appropriate to apply these to any engagement for which these assumptions were not designed.

In this engagement, we will need to do the same. A retail network in Arizona will have different economics from a retail network in New York, since the economic forces impacting them are different.

Moreover, even if we import the best practices from other parts of the world, we need to adjust and model them, since the forces impacting them are very different.

This is a key issue that we must think through and understand completely.

PAUSE & REFLECT

> What are the dangers of using analysis structures from other studies, even studies that appear to be answering the same question word for word?

> What are the risks in an approach that tests the client's intended strategy, rather than accepting it and helping them implement it?

> How should we mitigate those risks?

WEEK 0: PLANNING

STRATEGY

12. BASIC LOGIC CAN GENERATE AN 80%-ACCURATE ANSWER BEFORE DETAILED ANALYSIS IS REQUIRED.

Get comfortable using business judgment and logic to narrow the scope of the problem.

BANKING PRODUCTS

Each team member has called to see how they are preparing for the engagement. My main focus is to ensure everyone can read, manipulate, and model an income statement, cash flow statement, and balance sheet.

We spent a good seventy-five minutes talking Peter through what he expects from the case studies. We have high hopes for the work he will do.

We will refer to the independently owned businesses that borrow from LAB to lend to entrepreneurs as distribution financial intermediaries (DFIs), financial intermediaries, or retail financial intermediaries. In different parts of the world, they have different names.

LAB also distributes capital via other very small outlets, but we need to see the data to decide how to categorize those smaller outlets.

We also spoke to the client, Guillermo, who agreed with the rough changes we plan to present next week for the overall scope (boundaries of the engagement). But he kept coming back to the focus on the retail option. It is very clear the client believes the retail structure will work, since they are citing the success of the existing retailers, DFIs, which they do not own but which they lend money to, who in turn lend money to entrepreneurs in the US and Mexico.

We have been promised the financials of these DFIs who borrow from LAB to lend to the end-borrower. We are surprised that intermediaries they do not own are so open to sharing their financials.

Those financials better be audited. And not by an audit firm whose cousin is a relative of the DFI owner!

We will just have to see what the numbers say.

The client offers three major products:

1. Loans (debt instruments)
2. Equity investments (LAB will fund an entrepreneur by taking an equity stake in the business.)
3. Credit guarantees (LAB will guarantee the unsecured loans private banks offer to entrepreneurs). This is not available in the US. However, LAB will also guarantee the unsecured loan the DFIs issue to borrowers in Mexico who cross the border and open businesses in the United States.

Logic tells me the credit guarantee scheme is being abused due to moral hazard. What is the incentive for the banks to find worthy borrowers if the loan is guaranteed?

Of course, it depends on the percentage guaranteed.

The bigger the guarantee, the greater it will be abused. Hopefully, the pain is evenly shared between the bank and the distributors. In addition, this product is not clear to me. Why would a private bank push this product? What's in it for them? Our early guess is they are charging very large interest rates to make it worth their while.

STRATEGY

Although we are reporting directly to the CEO on this engagement, we have been assigned Guillermo, a very capable special projects manager, to serve as our direct liaison.

Guillermo is a forty-three-year-old veteran of LAB and a former McKinsey associate. He is thoughtful, sincere and very determined that the bank fulfills its mandate of creating jobs while building a sustainable business. He has expressed frustration with the slow pace at which the bank is moving and the poor results they have achieved.

Fraud is a problem, and he is convinced most of the numbers we are seeing in the industry will not pass a basic audit.

A skeptical client is a good client.

I think we are lucky to have such a committed person assigned to the engagement on a day-to-day basis. We spent most of this evening discussing his career aspirations and the future he sees for himself at the bank.

It also helps to have a client team that is committed, capable, and considered in their approach.

Seventeen days remain until we start the engagement. This weekend and most of next week I will lead the effort, to plan and structure the engagement. The overall approach needs to be fairly clear in my head before the team arrives.

In the final week before the engagement, we have set up an onboarding process for the team in order to teach them the core strategy skills needed. Then we have the weekend and the first day arrives in all its glory.

Millions will be impacted either way by our findings. They have to be right.

WEEK 0: PLANNING

PAUSE & REFLECT

> What are the dangers of a client team that is not skeptical?

> Why do we spend so much time planning the study, hypotheses and analyses?

> What benefits can we expect from such planning?

STRATEGY

13. ENSURE THAT THE CEO SMOOTHS THE PATH FOR THE CONSULTANTS.

Clients enjoy avoiding consultants unless they are told to cooperate.

INITIAL LETTER

Guillermo has started booking us focus interviews (see **Exhibit 11**). We must ensure all the stakeholders to whom we need to speak are on that list.

Below is the letter the LAB CEO is sending on our behalf to request the focus interviews:

> Dear Stella:
>
> El TORO FINANCIAL SERVICES ENGAGEMENT PARTICIPATION
>
> Latin America Bank (LAB) is actively pursuing means of better achieving its mandate. We must increase our effectiveness at lending to greater numbers of marginalized commercial borrowers while improving our risk management and collections. We appreciate your role in helping us achieve these aims.
>
> In order to further improve, LAB has recently engaged (Firm Name Here) to explore ways of accelerating progress in achieving our goals.
>
> We will be analyzing various stakeholder roles and positions during the engagement. As a valuable player, it is critical to better understand El Toro Financial Services.

STRATEGY

As part of the analysis of the current situation including successes and challenges, members of the engagement team would like to visit El Toro Financial Services during the next week. Team members would like to spend a full day analyzing typical daily operations. I would value your assistance in helping them arrange the necessary meetings and access.

Should you have any concerns or questions, please do not hesitate to contact Guillermo [redacted] or myself. Please be assured that all information will be kept strictly confidential and only used inside LAB.

This is an exciting period in LAB's growth. I am personally involved and committed to this engagement and believe its outcome is critical to our success.

Regards

Office of the CEO

El Toro is a key player. They are one of the largest distribution financial intermediaries (DFIs) funding entrepreneurs near the US-Mexican border. In essence, LAB believes El Toro is such a lucrative business, they want in on the action.

That is not the only reason. They also think El Toro is not funding enough entrepreneurs.

What if we find the opportunity south of the border is bigger than the opportunity north of the border? There may be 30 million unbanked entrepreneurs, but there is probably double that number in Mexico and with far less competition.

That said, our role is not to analyze the opportunity in Mexico, Central America, or elsewhere.

We need to determine if it is viable for LAB to enter the US through the creation of a retail branch network to provide financing for entrepreneurs, primarily immigrants, to start micro, small and medium-size businesses.

PAUSE & REFLECT

> How would you work with a client who does not think you have the CEOs support?

> Why do we prefer in-person focus interviews when technology would easily allow us to digitize and run the process remotely?

WEEK 0: PLANNING

STRATEGY

EXHIBIT 11: Focus Interview

LAB Focus Interview Questionnaire

LAB MARKET-ENTRY STRATEGY ENGAGEMENT

INSTITUTION AND DEPARTMENT _____
INTERVIEWER _____
INTERVIEWEE _____
DATE _____

INTRODUCTION

- Consultant Names
- FIRMSconsulting Engagement
- Project Overview
- Purpose of Interview

- Interview Method
- Note-taking
- Time Frame
- Confidentiality

PURPOSE OF INTERVIEW

LAB is actively pursuing means of better achieving its mandate. LAB aims to increase its effectiveness at lending to greater numbers of marginalized commercial borrowers while improving its risk management and collections. We appreciate your role in helping us achieve these aims.

In order to improve further, LAB has recently engaged FIRMSconsulting to explore ways of accelerating progress in achieving its goals. FIRMSconsulting was selected based on its local and international experience, and its understanding of LAB's requirements.

We will be analysing various stakeholders' roles and positions during the project. We regard your insights as valuable in helping us understand how to improve.

Should there be time constraints, prioritize the questions with two asterisks.

Definition of Development Finance Market for the purpose of the interview: Provision of services and loans to commercial entities that have struggled to obtain credit through traditional (formal) channels.

WEEK 0: PLANNING

Market Structure — SEGMENTS

1. Please identify clearly differentiated market segments in the development finance market. In microfinance in general, can you or how would you break them down into subsegments?

2. Please identify how the needs differ for each segment?

Market Structure (cont)

SEGMENTS

SEGMENTS	NEEDS

Market Structure (cont)

SEGMENTS

3. Can the needs of these segments be met through one value proposition (specific product, channel, service mix), or would any segments require a separate and specific focus? Could you elaborate on your answers?

4. For those that you think require specific value propositions, can you identify how these are currently being met? (Bank versus nonbank, community lending forums, credit unions, etc.)

Market Structure (cont)

SEGMENTS

5. Are there any segments where needs are not being met adequately? Elaborate.

6. For those segments where needs are not being met, do you think a feasible value proposition can be developed? Could you elaborate on your answers?

Institutional Successes

COMPANY ACTIVITIES

7. Do you believe your institution is fulfilling the needs of any of these segments to their maximum potential?**

8. What successes and failures have you had, and what do you ascribe these to?**

Market Economics — SUSTAINABILITY

9. Do you believe there is a minimum sustainable loan size for the development finance market? Why?**

   Yes ☐   No ☐

   If so, how much? (*Elaborate.*)**

   0–500 ☐   501–1,000 ☐   1,001–3,000 ☐

   3,001–5,000 ☐   5,001–10,000 ☐   10,000+ ☐

10. If more credit could be extended to the development finance market, how relevant would the following factors be in making this possible? Rank 1 through 5: 1 = not relevant at all, 5 = most relevant.**

	Not Relevant				Very Relevant
Better debt collection	1	2	3	4	5
More after-loan care	1	2	3	4	5
Stronger risk assessment	1	2	3	4	5
Low interest rates	1	2	3	4	5
Location	1	2	3	4	5
Stronger MIS	1	2	3	4	5
Other	1	2	3	4	5

LAB Effectivness

STRENGTHS WEAKNESSES OPPORTUNITIES THREATS (SWOT)

11. Are you aware of the products and services LAB provides?

    - Credit guarantee
    - Microcredit organization loans
    - Seed-funding disbursement
    - Ownership reform credit facility
    - Development financial intermediary loans
    - Equity funds
    - Mentorship

12. What do you believe LAB's mandate is?**

13. In which areas is LAB achieving its mandate, and where do you think it could improve?**

LAB Effectivness (cont)

(SWOT)

14. For those areas of potential improvement, why do you think LAB needs to improve its performance?**

15. How successful do you think the Development Financial Intermediary (small business and microlender) channel has been in helping LAB achieve its mandate?

16. How would you rate the level of opportunity for new players entering the development finance market, only in the US border states?

| No Opportunity ☐ | Little Opportunity ☐ |
| Medium Opportunity ☐ | Major Opportunity ☐ |

LAB Effectivness (cont)

(SWOT)

17. Why (and for where) do you say this?

18. Do you think there is room for LAB to play a more active role in the market? Why?**

19. How do you see LAB fitting in with other government (Latin and US) initiatives to stimulate development finance?

20. Could government efforts (Latin and US) be better coordinated? If so, how?

Closing

Thank you for your time. Is there anything else you would like to add that we have not covered?

May we call on you again if other questions arise?

14. FORGETTING THE EXPECTATIONS EXCHANGE IS PROBABLY THE SINGLE BIGGEST CAREER KILLER.

Most consultants end up with poor reviews since they just do not know any better.

WHY HAVE THE EXCHANGE?

The partner has to serve two roles in this engagement:

1. Managing the client and serving as the strategy and, to some extent, the subject matter expert.

2. A more important role is providing cover—like the way the air force protects ground troops—for the team so its members can go out and do the analyses required to test our hypotheses.

That latter role is more critical. No matter how well we manage the client, unless we have hard data to frame a very emotional topic, we will eventually lose credibility.

In military terms, you can think of the engagement team as the infantry unit. They are in the field, and the partner needs to let them do what they need to do.

The team only calls in air support if something goes very wrong. That is when they need to call in the partner. It is our job to make sure nothing goes so poorly that it impacts their ability to complete the analyses. That is the support I provide.

This is an important analogy to think about. If the partner were too close to the team, I would not train them to make decisions by themselves and they would not grow.

Worse, the partner wouldn't give the manager room to assert control of the engagement. So, she needs to suffer a few setbacks initially, then learn to adjust and grow into the role. This is the price to ensure that she is ready to manage the engagement in the more intellectually stressful parts from around Weeks 3 and 4.

That said, you will soon see that in all our engagements, Weeks 1 to 3 or 4 are usually the worst in terms of the pace we set.

FEEDBACK

Expectation exchanges from the team are starting to come in: We are glad to see they are so prompt. That is a good sign. Now, let's see if the content is thoughtful.

Associates:

1. We are not happy with these expectations. They show a lack of ambition for the two associates. We need to send a signal about what we expect through stated expectations. We are wary of interns who just want a learning experience. We are here to potentially change the face of small-business financing in the US. Merely "learning" is, at the very best, a mediocre objective.

2. This is not a typical internship. I will set up a call to make sure the associates understand how this engagement will be run. It will be the second call on the same topic.

3. It is best not to underestimate how entrenched myths are

about consulting and how many calls it takes to change them. It's those blogs written by associates who present distorted advice about what partners expect.

4. What I expect as a partner is very different from what an associate thinks I expect.

Manager:

1. The manager's expectations are good, but we sense a lack of confidence. A consulting internship is not where you go to find yourself. There is a very specific tell when someone does not believe in themselves because they believe no one believes in them.

> **Nimisha:** "I suppose you will be checking my work extensively?"
>
> **Partner:** "Not more than the rest of the team, and probably less."
>
> **N:** "Shouldn't I receive more guidance as the manager?"
>
> **P:** "No, you have so far shown all the signs that you are quite capable and have good management skills."
>
> **N:** "Really? What are those skills?
>
> That last question, is the tell.

2. We will also need to speak to her, but she probably just needs support and will be fine.

We will obviously adjust my expectations to accommodate the unique requirements of each person. But broadly speaking, this is what we want:

1. To guide and develop the younger team members
2. Total ownership of the problem statement and not the solution: Be accountable and not just responsible.
3. Be flexible on activities and show initiative.
4. Fail fast if you have to, though spend zero time apologizing or making excuses, and 100% of the time fixing the problem.
5. You will not be measured by your mistakes but how you respond to them.
6. Build good relationships with all stakeholders, including lower-level employees.
7. A policy of no surprises
8. Let's try to make this the most influential engagement ever done in the history of development finance. That means looking at what other consulting firms and the US government has already done for this banking client and setting a higher bar on the level of insight and helping the client.
9. Provide support and assistance to the other streams
10. Leave a legacy through this engagement and honor our values. What we will do will change the lives of millions of US immigrants and small-business owners, for better or worse. Many will not know who did the work, but they must know that a team took charge, and what they did on that day mattered.
11. Live our values. Leave if you cannot honor our values.

PAUSE & REFLECT

> Do you need to be accountable or responsible for your piece or work in an engagement?
> Does it matter?
> How would you use the expectations exchange to manage your manager and your direct report?
> Whom can you trust to show your lack of confidence and professional vulnerability?

STRATEGY

15. MOST HARD SKILLS ARE A COMMODITY IN MANAGEMENT CONSULTING.

The analytical process is crucial and not the analytical frameworks.

TRAINING

Now, we need to prepare the onboarding, which will happen the week before the engagement commences. That is exactly one week from now, since the engagement begins in two weeks.

It will be designed as a very consulting-focused MBA, and the partner will lead the training.

First, the agenda and then the content needs to be developed.

This is an important step that is hard to do, and many firms underinvest in this area.

If new consultants see the investment you make in them, they realize what they are doing matters.

The signals a partner, and firm, sends to consultants directly determine the way the consultants will act.

The training must focus on soft and hard skills (see **Exhibit 12**), such as:

1. Soft skills like speaking, writing, managing clients, presenting
2. Hard skills in two areas:
    a. Core skills like storyboarding, developing hypotheses, designing analyses, conducting focus interviews.

b. Noncore skills like the economics of retail finance, managing senior clients.

EXHIBIT 12: New consultants must master four foundational skills

Since the team focuses on breaking down the analyses, the partner is focused on the insights, a.k.a. putting it together with the EM

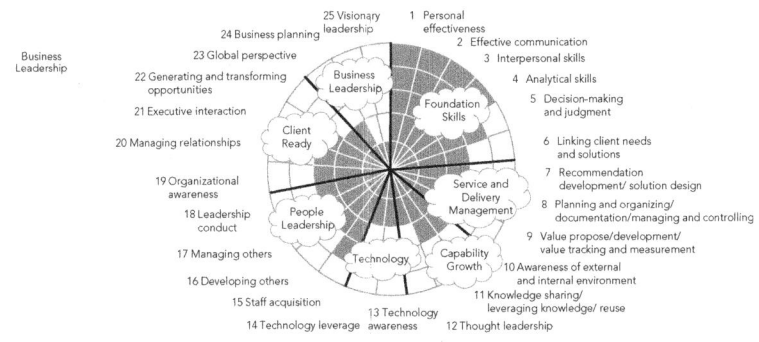

The team will first use our existing engagement training programs on StrategyTraining.com (A Typical McKinsey et al. Engagement) to prepare in their own time, and then I will take them through a live training session using a fictitious client. They will also read our books. Most of the preparation should be done online. The live session merely builds on what I already expect them to have mastered. These are the parts of the training I expect them to master:

WEEK 0: PLANNING

A Typical McKinsey, BCG, et al. Engagement: 1 Ready to Structure this Engagement[9]

A Typical McKinsey, BCG, et al. Engagement: 2 Ready to Develop the Work Streams[10]

A Typical McKinsey, BCG, et al. Engagement: 3 Ready to Plan the Work Streams[11]

21 Days, How to Develop Big Insights[12]

Titans of Strategy Series, How to Solve Big Problems[13]

How to Become a McKinsey Partner. 1st Time Ever Revealed.[14]

Reading: *Succeeding as a Management Consultant*, 2nd Ed.[15]

Reading: *The Strategy Journal*[16]

This may look like a lot, but they are fairly short programs that can be completed in a day. The books can be read in a week or so.

---

[9] https://www.strategytraining.com/mck-bcg-et-al-study-p1-ready-to-structure-the-study

[10] https://www.strategytraining.com/mck-bcg-et-al-study-p2-ready-to-develop-the-work-streams

[11] https://www.strategytraining.com/mck-bcg-et-al-study-p3-ready-to-plan-the-work-streams

[12] https://www.strategytraining.com/how-to-develop-big-insights

[13] https://www.strategytraining.com/how-to-solve-big-problems-with-ex-mckinsey-partner-kevin-p-coyne

[14] https://www.strategytraining.com/how-to-become-a-mckinsey-partner-first-time-revealed-full-program

[15] Safarova, Kris, *Succeeding as a Management Consultant*. 2nd ed., https://amzn.to/3a3atTn

[16] Safarova, Kris, *The Strategy Journal*, https://amzn.to/2QGft9d

Never outsource training externally or use junior employees. In consulting, the only real asset we have is the team and how they respond over the engagement's duration.

If a firm outsources training, then it implies the value of its asset is not differentiated. It must be differentiated and that implies only the most senior partners should do the training.

In the mentorship model, the secrets of the firm are passed from senior partner to future senior partner. When at the firm, the partner designed and led the training for corporate strategy and corporate finance. He, therefore, knew exactly what we were getting and how we were developing young associates and analysts.

It is tough to commit so much time to that cause, but it pays off in the long term.

No associates, no managers and certainly no external people should do the core training. They can help, but they cannot know enough to do this.

WEEK 0: PLANNING

PAUSE & REFLECT

> How have you personally been impacted by an underinvestment in training?

> What would you do differently if you have to develop training for your team, office, or firm?

> What percentage of training time should be spent on hard skills versus soft skills?

> Do you believe training can fully prepare a consultant for a real engagement?

> If not, what is the purpose of training?

STRATEGY

16. SMALL SIGNALS ON AN ENGAGEMENT SNOWBALL INTO SETTING THE TONE.

Think carefully about the tactical decisions made and the signals sent to the client and team.

ENGAGEMENT NAME

In large strategy engagements, the client and the firm like setting up an engagement name and logo.

This signifies the importance of what is being done.

This usually happens on massive transformation engagements where we will have to get a large percentage of the employee base to support an idea. It is less common on pure corporate strategy and business-unit strategy engagements, where we typically only engage very senior executives.

LAB, however, believes the retail structure entry model is feasible and is already thinking about implementation.

We selected the name Project Independencia.

It is a good name because it shows the bank is focused on the thing that matters most to them: their clients, who are micro, small, and medium-size business borrowers.

They are not internally focused and want their clients to achieve financial independence from the funding LAB provides. This is a good sign that they are naming the engagement to signify benefits to their borrowers.

If they picked a name like Project Profits, or something like that, then we would be worried. That name would signal that they're very short-term focused on their own benefits. If they serve their clients, well then profits will be a by-product of the process.

EXPENSE BUDGET SIGNALS

We have repeatedly stressed that a case team will do great things on an engagement, if you select them through a very thorough recruitment process and, thereafter, treat them like they are about to do great things.

Do not expect consultants to change the world if you treat them like people who are average.

This comes down to selecting hotel accommodation, airline seats, and laptop accessories, which signify the consultants are important. They should not travel economy class, should stay in good hotels and should receive superior amenities. All of this builds up to signal to the consultants that they are not ordinary, and extraordinary things will be expected of them.

How do you do this? By negotiating a very large expense budget for the engagement.

The partner has taken the liberty of negotiating a better expense budget than he used as a partner at the firm. He could do this since we have a lower overhead structure and could move more of the budget to expenses.

Strategy consultants will in the long-term struggle to operate in the C-Suite if they do not believe they belong in the C-Suite.

Note that this does not mean we will waste the client's money. We are vetting expenses on the engagement, and we will carefully check receipts. However, the team must be treated based on the value we expect them to generate.

WEEK 0: PLANNING

Make no mistake, they will work like they have not worked before and make an impact they have not made before. The least we can do is treat them well during that time.

You will be surprised how people rise to the occasion if you behave like you expect them to rise to the occasion. We will constantly drive them to do better, improve the analyses and results, but we will support them.

A good research and formatting back office is critical, and other areas in which we will invest significantly. Yes, it's true. We do not do all the slides ourselves. That is why they look so good.

I expect consultants to have the ability to produce beautiful slides, but we will use an engagement coordinator to make sure everything looks good. The coordinator we will use is an ex-BCG designer who now lives in Romania and is an ideal seven hours ahead of us.

The plan is to send her the designs and pencil sketches when we leave, and she will do them overnight and email them back by 7 a.m. ET.

Given the sensitivity of the material we are using, we will only use a coordinator we know well. Please do not try to replicate this step by finding someone on the internet. And remember to ensure that you follow all required procedures as it relates to protecting the client's confidentiality.

Freelance sites are generally not the place to find coordinators. It's not that there are no good people there. They are just very hard to find, and it can be a painful trial and error process.

Confidentiality is the issue.

Typically, an engagement team will spend Fridays at the office working on internal projects and attending to firm issues. They will not be at the client's offices. Given the nature of this engagement and the fact that there is no value in being at the office, I am going to use the same model but make some changes:

1. The team will work half-days on Friday.

2. They will work at the hotel for the rest of the day.

3 The second half of the day will be focused on internal issues we may be having on the engagement, catching up, and the like.

Given that this client uses other consultants for lots of their other work, the client would be well aware that we need to work off-site one day a week.

PAUSE & REFLECT

> How do you feel when you are working long hours on a tough engagement, but your firm is unable or unwilling to spend money on better food, travel, or accommodation?

> Does it lower your morale, enthusiasm, and work quality?

> What changes can you realistically ask your firm to make?

> How can expenses be managed to improve the well-being of the consultants so that their output materially improves?

STRATEGY

17. PARTNERS EXPECT EFFICIENCY AND SELFLESSNESS WHEN COMMUNICATING.

Communicate in a way that makes it easy for partners to complete their work, not your work. This is a key mindset change.

EFFICIENT COMMUNICATION

When writing to partners, or anyone for that matter, be action oriented and focused. Long emails will not get read.

This is how we wrote emails as associates:

> Title: Decision needed on focus interviews by 5 p.m. Monday
>
> Tom,
>
> The client wants an update on the draft focus interviewee list by 5 p.m. Monday.
>
> I am not sure if we need to add the competitors, we wanted to interview in the draft list I sent. I think we should. Respond if you disagree.
>
> Thanks, X

In other words, let the client know in the title what he or she is opening, and add a deadline so we know whether we can read it later. Also, make it easy for the recipient not to have to respond. Here, the recipient only needs to respond if he or she disagrees. And the email already offers a solution, so the recipient doesn't need to think much. It does not ask what to do. And it allows the response to be a simple yes or no. This is very efficient.

STRATEGY

Also, don't leave cryptic voice messages on the phone. Is there anything worse than long, unstructured, vague voice messages?

Yes.

Vague voicemails.

Never leave a voice saying you need to discuss something urgently and then fail to tell someone what that is!

If you don't tell me the purpose in the voice message, we will need to:

1. See the flashing icon on our phone.
2. Pick it up.
3. Excuse ourselves from the meeting, since we cannot determine if your agenda is more important than the meeting.
4. Check our messages.
5. Call you since we cannot deduce if the subject is important.
6. Call you since I cannot type my response given that you did not tell me what you want to discuss.
7. Then take time discussing something that may not turn out to be important.

Leave a message stating the problem. Better yet, send an email like the one above.

This is about being productive and efficient, and respecting other people's time. Time is tight on a strategy engagement, and vague voicemails and emails are a luxury no one can afford.

As a partner, I managed seven engagements simultaneously, at the relationship level, in the worst months and five at once in the average months. You cannot imagine what it must be like getting cryptic messages from team members across seven different studies and multiple time zones, all speaking different languages. The phone dies by 2 p.m., just from the incessant beeping and blinking!

We think overseeing so many studies are too much. It is tough to really generate value for a client if the partner is overseeing more than three engagements, thought there may be up to five smaller engagements within each of those.

Therefore, we are spending most of this week wrapping up other tasks so we can fully commit our time to the financial services engagement and upcoming electricity engagement.

PAUSE & REFLECT

> Did you notice a positive change when trying the communication approach above?
> What are the principles of this communication approach?
> How can you apply these principles to other parts of your communication and/or career?

WEEK 0: PLANNING

18. FOCUS INTERVIEWS ARE THE HEART OF TOP-DOWN ANALYSES AND MUST BE DONE FIRST.

Focus interviews are critical to quickly testing initial hypotheses and onboarding the team in a safe environment.

ENGAGEMENT PLAN

It's crucial to book the dates for updates as soon as the engagement commences. Otherwise, the client's diary may not be free.

We have built a rough engagement plan and believe the following is feasible. We will confirm this once the team begins on the first day. The client and team need to be comfortable with the timing we are proposing.

For now, Guillermo will hold these slots in all participant diaries.

> Week 2: Progress update
>
> Week 3: Case study findings and market segment analyses
>
> Week 4: Focus interview feedback, modeling report, value chain and competitor analyses, and identifying the business model options
>
> Week 6: Is market entry viable and what do we propose next? (We will have the answer much earlier and discuss the findings, but we will formally present the recommendation here.)
>
> Week 8: Board presentation: our recommended option, analyses of the loan book, and US pilot site recommendations.

Week 9: Final report with detailed analyses supporting the recommendation.

How did we perform these analyses for each update so early? We did not get the analyses out of thin air.

Here is a rough breakdown of the steps taught above:

1. Determine the objective function we will maximize (the problem we will solve).
2. Determine the drivers of the objective function.
3. Prioritize the drivers.
4. Break down the prioritized drivers.
5. Repeat this process until we have a decision tree about four to five levels down.
6. Built hypotheses for the prioritized branches.
7. Design the analyses we would need to test the hypotheses.
8. Determine the likely finding from each analysis.
9. Take all the likely findings and lay them out like a story.
10. Determine if the story is compelling. Is it worth doing all this work for this story?

This is how we knew what work needed to be done. We will repeat this process with the team so the members can learn how it should be done during a real engagement.

It's best not to do an analysis just because it is part of some checklist. That is not a strategy. It is wasting time.

An analysis must only be done to test a hypothesis, the hypothesis must come from the decision tree, and the decision tree must come from a clear objective function for the engagement.

Everything flows naturally from the other.

At this stage, we have twenty-nine focus interviews planned. The length of the list could go up a little or even down a little as diaries change, but it looks like a good start.

It is unusual to have so much planning and coordination support from a client over a week before the engagement starts. But Guillermo and the CEO have pushed hard to create space for us to do this.

The majority of the interviews are with banks that distribute LAB's wholesale products through their retail branch network.

The credit guarantee scheme will be carefully reviewed in these focus interviews, since LAB is rather proud of this product and believes it is a win-win situation for the local banks.

We have several development finance experts to interview, including a few from Yale and Harvard located in Africa and Latin America.

Of course, as the majority shareholder of LAB, the government will be interviewed.

SHADOW STUDIES

You will notice none of the distribution financial intermediaries are being interviewed. We have a very special plan for them.

For the DFIs and recipients of the funding (entrepreneurs), we will be spending a day or two shadowing them silently, with their consent, to see what they do, why they do it, and how it impacts the economics of the business. We will do a time analysis.

This is probably one of the best parts of the engagement.

If the team needs help on the ground, we will personally volunteer to shadow a food entrepreneur and taste the excellent Latin cuisine.

The team will fan out across New York, California, Nevada, New Mexico, Arizona, and Florida to conduct the shadow studies and focus interviews. In total, we want to cover nine southern states. New York is being added as a control location.

Texas is not yet on the list due to scheduling problems, but we hope to correct that soon.

Imagine spending a hot summer in California shadowing entrepreneurs. There will be many shadows due to the blazing hot sunlight.

Obviously, the team needs to be dressed appropriately for the role.

A Brooks Brothers chinos-clad consultant in the middle of an informal LA food market in a seedy part of town is just asking to be mugged!

In those situations, jeans and a T-shirt are the norm. We are visiting 2 DFIs and will spend over a day at each.

One is a DFI offering entrepreneurs funding of $700 and only targets customers within a cluster, such as focusing on clients who operate on the same street. There are many different types of clusters.

Another is a massive operation offering funding for established small businesses that are two years old or more, with an average business loan size of $50,000.

We will split the time at each DFI as follows:

1. Day 1: We will go out with a loan officer and see how she or he spends her day visiting clients, following up on delinquent loans, and following the general routine.

2. Day 2: We will spend a day in the office seeing how the key processes work, map the processes and time them. The processes we will map include processing a funding request, updating a customer file, adjusting a loan request, handling delinquencies, and more.

Both DFIs are within driving distance of the US-Mexican border.

These are my early thoughts, but if we assume LAB wants to replicate the retail structure in the US because LAB thinks the DFIs are successful, then we need to test for this.

Are the DFIs successful, and if they are, under what conditions are they successful and can LAB replicate these conditions?

KEY CONSIDERATIONS

The team should understand the following from the focus interviews and shadow studies:

1. Operational issues and requirements for successful microlending in the US and Mexico
2. Business model structures and products/services offered
3. Customer needs, customer support needs, and how these vary by business, industry type and loan size
4. Systems, loan book, people, and organization structure requirements for different loan sizes and target markets in different states, for different sectors across different customer profiles

5. Economics of the value chain: margins, costs, prices.

6. Lessons each DFI learned in starting up.

How forthcoming will the DFIs be? LAB does not own them. They are clients of LAB, the retailers to LAB's wholesaler role.

Will they share the information we need?

We think they will. From this information, we can deduce what we need to model this operation correctly, and since LAB will have a lending-side mirror of the loan book managed by the DFI, we can double-check the numbers.

PAUSE & REFLECT

> Have you tried using focus interviews at the start of an engagement?
> How did the engagement change by adding this step?
> What challenges would we face if we skipped the focus interviews?

WEEK 0: PLANNING

19. ARE YOU DESIGNING A CASE STUDY ABOUT A COMPANY OR AN ATTRIBUTE?

Case studies are probably the most misunderstood and poorly done part of strategy studies.

DESIGNING CASE STUDIES

We will be preparing detailed case studies of quite a few development finance banks. We have some strict rules for this. These rules ensure we are carefully separating the glossy marketing spin from the facts using tools like this:

1. Ensure an equal balance of success and failure cases.

2. Limited third-party information in newspaper articles, press releases, magazines, or business school case studies can be used, unless they are corroborated through a focus interview, which we conduct, with someone senior from the organization under discussion.

3. Either a past employee and/or a peer in the industry must corroborate all focus interviews findings.

4. Data and facts must be corroborated by at least two interviewees.

5. We will not do case studies of entire companies, but rather specific assets / competencies / initiatives / problems within companies.

These guidelines ensure we do not merely follow shoddy reporting in the press.

Given the rigor that we are using, this implies we will do fewer case studies but extract far more useful insights.

The team will do a first cut using media information, and we will use that to decide which development finance banks and agencies will be analyzed via in-person interviews.

We have decided to proceed with seven first-cut case studies using publicly available information.

From that initial list, we will likely pare down the list to three or four detailed case studies.

This is the initial draft of case studies for the engagement. This may change later once the team settles in and we know more from the focus interviews that guide our thinking on where the best ideas are.

Peter is leading this work and will also need to create a set of criteria for choosing the focus interviews. He may very well produce a new list based on his more-refined ranking system.

This is where we will focus the first cut:

1. Mexico
2. Brazil
3. India
4. Dominican Republic
5. Kenya
6. Thailand
7. Bangladesh

PAUSE & REFLECT

> Do you feel case studies generate genuine insights?
> What is the value of a case study?
> Are they used merely to reinforce the consultant's initial ideas?

WEEK 0: PLANNING

20. DOES YOUR VALUE SYSTEM EXIST AS WORDS OR IN EVERYDAY ACTIONS?

Think carefully of things you take for granted that may be damaging or discriminatory.

WORDS VS. ACTIONS

It is critical to ensure that interns understand why our value system and culture are the source of our strength and why the work they do matters. We do this in several ways, and you can do the same:

1. Every intern receives copies of our exclusively made and designed journals, including the Strategy Journal[17], Strategic Business Case Journal and Market Entry Strategy Journals. These journal were developed over ten years ago, and many of our clients use it on a daily, weekly, and monthly basis as a step-by-step guide to solving difficult business problems. Inside, the book includes a personal note from our presiding partner explaining our values. It sometimes surprises clients when they pick up the book and see this list of values.

2. We expect the interns to use the Strategy Journal as their primary daily tool and guide. It was designed for the most complex engagements.

3. We forbid sexist images. Lots of companies use male symbols like ties and men's suits to denote business. We do not allow this anywhere.

---

[17] Safarova, Kris, *The Strategy Journal*, https://amzn.to/2QGft9d

4. We do not like apologies. When someone apologizes or makes excuses, it implies they have stopped fixing the problem. It is more important to fix the problem. If you fix the problem, an apology is unnecessary.

We also maintain excessive client confidentiality in these ways:

1. Within the firm, a partner not working on an engagement will have limited access to the engagement materials. They will get or may request access to a sanitized version only.

2. We air gap laptops with sensitive data. This means they have not been connected to the internet and will not be connected to the internet.

3. We are forbidden from disclosing the name of a former client, even if the client gives us permission to do so.

4. We do not use past client details in proposals.

5. We do not offer testimonials and referrals since this would mean disclosing client details.

6. Interns and employees sign an extensive and far-reaching NDA and confidentiality agreement similar to the one Rumpelstiltskin had a mother sign.

7. We do not solicit work. It must be referred to us.

This extreme focus on client confidentiality is one reason we can handle sensitive engagements. The client knows we disclose nothing—ever.

The onboarding of interns will take place over the three days immediately preceding the engagement. I wanted to do it over four days, but because the interns are returning from many far-flung lands after their MBA travels, some downtime seemed wise. I do not want jet-lagged interns in an onboarding session. That would be unkind to them.

PAUSE & REFLECT

> How do you feel when a firm's values do not match its actions?

> How do you feel when a firm's remuneration and bonus criteria do not match its values?

> What are good and bad values?

STRATEGY

WEEK 0: PLANNING

21. INTERNAL STRATEGY UNITS SOMETIMES FEEL CHALLENGED BY EXTERNAL CONSULTANTS.

Most internal units, however, understand they will not be involved in undertaking critical studies.

UNFORESEEN CHALLENGE

The internal strategy unit continues planning the rollout of the retail structure to replace the DFIs. There is no evidence LAB can compete economically in the US market.

This is at the core of what our engagement is trying to determine.

What happens if the strategy unit wants us to report to them? They are trying to co-opt the engagement by requiring that we report to them. As politely as possible, we must explain this is not possible since we were mandated by the CEO's office.

In fact, Guillermo will manage this since he represents the CEO's office, and we would prefer not to get involved in turf wars. It is not for us to manage the internal reporting structures.

As it stands, we liaise with Guillermo and report to the CEO's office. In our opinion, the engagement should not report to a unit that has a preconceived notion of what the answer should be.

The phone bill is about to set new records. We believe in calling people when we need things or to get a sense of how the team is doing. As the team prepares to arrive for their onboarding, we will speak to them often.

While at the firm, the partner often had very high phone bills for this very same reason.

In our discussions with the team, it appears the US market-entry decision is positioned incorrectly. It is not about helping people, because that is charity. This is about an economic opportunity, and that is how it should be presented. We cause more damage when we present it as a social issue.

Most of the weekend will be spent preparing for the onboarding and finalizing the materials and social events for the interns.

TIGHTENING THE SCOPE

In many ways, we are still adjusting the letter of proposal. We submitted the changes yesterday via email, and we expect today's meeting to be a formality.

The proposal essentially focuses all of the first few weeks on making a nuanced but important distinction in the following ways:

1. The first phase will not just examine the attractiveness of the US market.

2. We feel that is the incorrect question to answer. The US market could very well be attractive, but that does not imply it is attractive to the client.

3. The first part of the engagement will, therefore, determine whether retail structures within the US market are viable for the client. If they are not economically profitable (viable), then there is no point in examining the attractiveness of the US market.

… WEEK 0: PLANNING …

4. The second part will be determined based on whether the retail structures are viable. If they are viable, then we proceed with pilot implementation planning.

Once this foundation is agreed to, we have the final approval to commence. Then there is just a week to go.

CLIENT'S INTERESTS FIRST

How do we place the client's interests first? This is the central question I pretty much think about all the time in designing the engagement.

We need to ensure the engagement is not only of unimpeachable quality but actually provides a recommendation that is in the interest of the shareholders.

In many ways, how do we leave a legacy of values, quality, and insights?

We routinely contrast this to the internal work being done at LAB. It is about the way we respond to things.

For example, the internal strategy unit (ISU) decided after our appointment to present a new report to make their case. The ISU has started putting together a new report to explain the "solid benefits case" of entering the US market via retail channels.

Is this a good thing? Yes.

Most consulting firms worry when another firm or ISU challenges them. If you think about this carefully, you'll see it is good for the CEO to see two different views. Our job is not to win, whatever that might mean, but to present the best strategy for the client.

What other units or firms do is not important to us. If our work is correct, it will show.

STRATEGY

There is no need for any political machinations or movements.

We trust in the power of our work to stand for itself, coupled with our communication skills and relationship with the LAB leadership team.

And if the ISU finds flaws in our work, then that is a problem with our work, not with the ISU.

PAUSE & REFLECT

> How do you react when you are challenged by client employees?
> If you were to become defensive, would this help you?
> How do you manage a situation where you are sincerely doing what is in the client's best interests, but the client is unhappy?

STRATEGY

22. MILITARY STRATEGY TEACHES MUCH ABOUT COMPETITION STRATEGY.

The challenge, however, is in drawing the right conclusions.

REQUIRED READING

We use many military and sports lessons to train consultants in corporate strategy and strategy in general. In fact, at the firm we had a strategy theory initiative to extract lessons from military campaigns.

Two famous military campaigns indicate how to use your supposed disadvantage to your advantage. The interns are reading them.

These are quite dense to read on Wikipedia but important and useful:

1. Operation Barbarossa[18]
2. Napoleon's invasion of Russia[19]

Some key lessons are summarized below, though this is worth reading if you want to be a serious strategist:

1. Technical superiority means little if you can raise vast new resources quickly.
2. Supply chain management is vital.
3. Prepare for a campaign of attrition since things tend to take longer than expected.

---

[18] https://en.wikipedia.org/wiki/Operation_Barbarossa

[19] https://en.wikipedia.org/wiki/French_invasion_of_Russia

4. Mislead the enemy by abandoning what they think is important to you.

5. Make changes before there is a need to make changes.

STUDYING COMPETITIVE ADVANTAGE IS LIKE PHYSICS

The problem with studying the competitive position of the bank's competitors is we are examining what they are doing right now, when the client bank is not in the market.

However, if or when the bank enters, the competitors will move, morph, and display new skills. In strategy, it is important to predict what these skills will be and what actions the competitors will take.

This is similar to Heisenberg's uncertainty principle[20]: One cannot know the precise position and momentum of an atomic particle.

Why? The act of observing the particle means you need to "shine a light" on the particle, which imparts some energy to the particle, thereby shifting its momentum. So, what you are seeing is just after the light hits the particle, but we don't know where the particle will go just after that photo is taken. It's like taking a photo of a car as soon as you hit the gas. In a few seconds, the car will be somewhere else.

We want to see what happens after the light hits the particle.

Competitive strategy is very similar. Think of LAB's entry into the US as the light. We want to see how competitors will react after the bank enters the market because the competitors before and after market entry are very different animals.

---

[20] https://en.wikipedia.org/wiki/Uncertainty_principle

Bruce Henderson of BCG describes this concept very well using a marble analogy.[21]

So how do you get LAB's competitors to show their hand? If you can do that, that is good strategy planning.

Most competitive strategy famously and incorrectly looks at how competitors will use their strengths.

We are interested in how the bank's competitors will use their weaknesses.

This is important.

The words "strength" and "weakness" are terms that an external observer will assign to a set of attributes. However, just because we consider an attribute a weakness does not mean it is actually a weakness.

We need to think about how the competitor will use said attribute(s) to compete against the client.

History is littered with so-called weaknesses being deployed in an unexpected manner to rout a challenger.

We need to think without bias. We need to think like the competitors, something like this:

1. How are they deploying resources?
2. Where are resources fixed?
3. How responsive are they?
4. Why do they value certain parts of their operations?

---

[21] https://www.youtube.com/watch?v=YmZjJxS-Mw4

5. What happens when they are challenged?
6. How many of our assumptions about the bank's competitors confirm our bias?
7. Why do we have these biases?
8. What is the value of having these biases?

Most people have biases since they are too lazy to carefully check things.

We spent a long day at LAB meeting some of the executives and had a long lunch with Guillermo discussing the engagement, ISU engagement, changes at LAB, and pressure from the bank's majority shareholder.

As much as possible, we limited meetings since we wanted the engagement team to be with the partner as he meets executives.

PAUSE & REFLECT

> How are you analyzing competitive advantage?
> Are you applying a framework?
> How do you know the insights are correct?
> How do you know what is a competitive advantage or a disadvantage?

STRATEGY

WEEK 0: PLANNING

23. DEMONSTRATED COMPETENCY IS AT THE HEART OF THE BEST CONSULTING.

This explains why so many MBAs from the best programs end up disappointed: They expect the school name to carry them.

VIRTUAL TRAINING

We are piloting a virtual onboarding for the interns, followed by a live onboarding. Interns will prepare with the following programs.

- A Typical McKinsey, BCG, et al. Engagement: 1. Ready to Structure this Engagement[22]
- A Typical McKinsey, BCG, et al. Engagement: 2. Ready to Develop the Work Streams[23]
- A Typical McKinsey, BCG, et al. Engagement: 3. Ready to Plan the Work Streams[24]
- 21 Days, How to Develop Big Insights[25]

---

[22] https://www.strategytraining.com/mck-bcg-et-al-engagement-p1-ready-to-structure-the-engagement

[23] https://www.strategytraining.com/mck-bcg-et-al-engagement-p2-ready-to-develop-the-work-streams

[24] https://www.strategytraining.com/mck-bcg-et-al-engagement-p3-ready-to-plan-the-work-streams

[25] https://www.strategytraining.com/how-to-develop-big-insights

- How to Solve Problems, with an ex-McKinsey Strategy Practice Worldwide Co-Leader[26]
- How to Become a McKinsey Partner. 1st Time Ever Revealed, with ex-McKinsey Strategy Practice Worldwide Co-Leader[27]
- Reading: *Succeeding as a Management Consultant*, 2nd Ed.[28]
- Reading: *The Strategy Journal*[29]

The plan is for them to learn the basics via the online material, and we can focus on the more complex, practical, and realistic material in the live sessions.

We will balance theory with practical steps so that come the onboarding next week, they have the ability to simply start the engagement.

However, it will be fairly difficult for interns to pick up all the skills merely by watching the videos. They need to learn how to apply those skills on the job. Watching training materials will probably get them to about a 70% increase in skills. The books are equally meaningful—both *Succeeding as a Management Consultant* and *The Strategy Journal*. Careful and thoughtful reading of the books alongside the videos will lead to close to 90% mastery of the skills. But the repeated and regular application of what they learned is crucial to take them to 100% mastery.

---

[26] https://www.strategytraining.com/how-to-solve-big-problems-with-ex-mckinsey-partner-kevin-p-coyne

[27] https://www.strategytraining.com/how-to-become-a-mckinsey-partner-first-time-revealed-full-program

[28] Safarova, Kris, *Succeeding as a Management Consultant*, 2nd ed., https://amzn.to/3a3atTn

[29] Safarova, Kris, *The Strategy Journal*, https://amzn.to/2QGft9d

Plus, interns will need to watch me as I train them on the actual engagement. Certain things can be read and understood but putting them into practice is a slightly different story.

It's like driving. You can perfectly understand the driver's manual, but driving is quite a different issue.

NIMISHA'S DEMONSTRATED COMPETENCY

I expected some chatter from the team since Nimisha is not an MBA student at Harvard, Wharton, Stanford, INSEAD, Ivey, Columbia, Stern, Booth, Yale, Cornell, Duke, Darden, MIT or the like. She is at a school ranked on the fringes of the top twenty.

In fact, she is the youngest member of the team.

She has an accounting background.

The two associates are older, fit the stereotypical consulting backgrounds and probably see themselves as better choices to be the engagement manager.

However, selection is based on demonstrated competency; it is not based on paper competency.

Nimisha was by far the best applicant at demonstrating all the value-based, technical, and communication skills to lead a consulting team.

This is a key lesson about life and consulting: Having fantastic credentials only gets you the interview. Once you get the interview, your demonstrated competency matters.

MODELING THE SECTOR

Getting a big picture view of immigrant small-business entrepreneurship is pretty tough.

There are numerous studies heralding immigrants who start business. However, these studies tend to be biased towards:

1. Technology start-ups
2. Large and scalable businesses
3. Educated immigrants

It is difficult to assess the state of entrepreneurship among less-educated immigrants starting small businesses. Unfortunately, this is the view we need. LAB is not interested in funding the next Uber.

The bank's key strength is in understanding the risk profile and loan delinquency rate of low-income-survivalist borrowers in Mexico.

The model doing these calculations is largely built using data from the Mexican operations. How relevant will that model be for the US, where the drivers of behavior are very different?

We spent all day reading the annual reports of the various microfinance banks we would want to showcase in case studies. We are sure of this: The accounting standards are not great.

Most of the documents are mere marketing jobs versus careful analyses of the finances.

Many of the companies do not appear to track the number of the jobs they create. Those reports that do capture the information are really focusing on anecdotal evidence.

This is the problem with the sector; it does not easily stand up to rigorous analyses. Be cautioned, though, that this is just based on our initial reading. More work will need to be done to justify this view.

Even famous case studies present evidence that is really tough to corroborate. Do we listen to them, knowing it could be wrong, and make a multimillion decision to invest in the US?

No. That would be bad for the client.

We need a way to corroborate the job creation numbers without relying on a source that is incentivized to positively spin the numbers.

I can see that I am going to be very intimately involved in the case study analyses. More than I am normally involved.

Yet it is very fascinating at a personal level.

We saw a 90-year-old Chinese lady who runs a food stall and moves all the produce herself. She has no children, and her husband is deceased. She has no way of funding her business. If you sit in the same intersection throughout the day, you will see her walking up to four times in a single day to buy produce to replenish her stall. She closes her stall, locks it up, and then walks about 2 kilometers to pick up her produce.

Should she be funded? Will LAB benefit from such investments? What is the economic impact to the United States of helping her fund her business?

Should we worry about the overall economic impact on the US?

Once we review LAB's business in the US and Mexico, this is what we hypothesize we will find:

1. The DFIs probably are the most effective channels to distribute loans to create jobs.

2. The DFIs are probably also the most profitable business (all the literature points to this) since they must be pushing significant loan volume off a very low-cost structure.

3. Credit guarantees, where LAB backs loans offered by other banks, must be growing but losing money due to moral hazard.

4. LAB is surely running low on cash; the credit guarantees must lead to a large contingent liability on the balance sheet, which is tying up capital. LAB must be seeking a way to raise capital to pursue the US market.

5. LAB's funds are likely not earning a real economic profit. Their net operating profit after subtracting the cost of capital is probably negative.

6. LAB's real rate of return is probably slightly negative. If it were highly negative, we would be doing the corporate strategy for LAB and not merely looking at the market entry options.

These are all very early and rough hypotheses. Time will tell if we are right.

PAUSE & REFLECT

> Do you have different hypotheses for LAB?
> If they differ from our hypotheses, why do you think this is the case?
> Would you change the engagement approach at this stage?

STRATEGY

24. COMPETITION STRATEGY IS PARTIALLY ABOUT FORCING YOUR COMPETITORS TO WASTE RESOURCES ON PREEMPTING AN ACTION YOU WILL NOT TAKE.

Misdirection is a critical skill in business.

MENTORING NIMISHA

Nimisha and I will have a call tomorrow to ensure she is crystal clear about the Ranatunga Doctrine and how we plan to run things. As our engagement manager, she needs to both understand and be able to execute my pace for the engagement.

We want to impress upon her the need to very carefully analyze LAB's financials. No matter what the client says, we will find things they did not expect nor see in their very own numbers.

We just need to be careful about not falling for conventional wisdom and verifying things.

A lot will depend on the top-down financial analyses and focus interviews.

BATTLE OF DIEN BIEN PHU

The call went relatively well. She was able to quickly zoom in on the main issue. It went something like this:

Nimisha: If we are running things so fast, what are the lead indicators we are on track?

Partner: What do you mean?

N: We need to deliver a lot of insights by the second week. So, what must we have done by the Monday, Wednesday, and Friday of the first week?

P: Let's take the focus interviews. What do you think we need for them in the first week?

N: You said we need hypotheses. We need the draft interviews. We need a list of interviewees. We need the interviews to be set up. I think that is all.

P: That's good. Just break it down through all the steps so you are not surprised:

> Monday, you need all hypotheses by all streams.
>
> Monday, you need to finish the draft of the interview email invitation that the client will send out.
>
> Monday, you need to finish the list of interviewees.
>
> Tuesday, you need to have the hypotheses highlighted that can be tested in the interviews, and you need to adjust the interviews to incorporate those questions.
>
> Tuesday, you need to have the partner's sign-off and to plan the logistics.
>
> Wednesday, we need Guillermo to agree and book everything.

WEEK 0: PLANNING

> Thursday, you need to find backup interviewees for those who cannot or do not want to be interviewed.
>
> Next week, you need a process to collect feedback and define the hypotheses.
>
> This is not the exact process since Guillermo has already started, but you need to be thinking ahead at this level of operational detail. For each major task, it's about planning the task and having the time and space to pull the findings back into the study.
>
> **N:** Yes, I can do that. And I can lead this.
>
> **P:** I know you can do it. And there is nothing that can happen that is so bad that we cannot fix it. Don't forget that.

As a partner, it is tough to balance being supportive and making sure the engagement manager does not see this as a chance to "find" herself or himself. This may be the biggest problem with consultants who lack confidence.

If you are too friendly with them, many assume they should share their most pressing problems in life. Of course, there is a time for that, but that is not the main purpose of the engagement. I really don't need to know about the trauma of her first teenage kiss. That is going to give me my own nightmares.

The client's problems come first.

Nimisha is quite balanced in this regard. She can be personable but also highly professional.

The partner has two ways of communicating a point to the team: directly or indirectly.

STRATEGY

If there's time and you want a point to stick, make the indirect point through a business or military story.

Nimisha and I discussed the famous Battle of Dien Bien Phu[30] this morning. This is one of the most significant modern battles, and many armies fighting an insurgency or guerilla army have studied it.

Why did we discuss this battle? Because it changed the course of history.

> Military historian Martin Windrow wrote that Dien Bien Phu was "the first time that a non-European colonial independence movement had evolved through all the stages from guerrilla bands to a conventionally organized and equipped army able to defeat a modern Western occupier in pitched battle."

That single battle changed the course of every colony around the world from Africa to Asia:

> He added, "France's defeat in Indochina, coupled with the German destruction of French armies just fourteen years earlier, seriously damaged France's prestige elsewhere in its colonial empire, as well as with its NATO allies, chiefly with the United States. Within her empire, the defeat in Indochina served to spur independence movements in other colonies, notably the North African territories from which many of the troops who fought at Dien Bien Phu had been recruited. In 1954, six months after the battle at Dien Bien Phu ended, the Algerian War started, and by 1956, both [the] Moroccan and Tunisian protectorates had gained [their] independence."

---

[30] https://en.wikipedia.org/wiki/Battle_of_Dien_Bien_Phu

The Vietnamese under Võ Nguyên Giáp did exactly what the Russians did to the Germans during WWII:

1. The French, like the Germans, underestimated their enemies.

2. The French assumed the Vietnamese would not stage a direct assault. It was the Viet Cong's main weakness.

3. Like the Russians, the Vietnamese did exactly what the French were not expecting.

Why discuss Dien Bien Phu? The problem with discussing business strategy using business examples is that young consultants tend to be preprogrammed to discuss finances, Porter's theories, and the like, without forcing themselves to think about what it means. Strategy is about more than numbers. It is about intent, emotions, confidence, and more.

In other words, they use terms without truly understanding the meaning. They can sometimes sound smart without actually thinking.

Preprogrammed action is the curse of management consulting. Muscle-memory can lead to poor analyses.

By shifting the discussion to military strategy, the consultant cannot rely on preplanned catch phrases or vague generalizations. They are forced to think about the reasons.

Nimisha needs to really think about the underlying concepts and how they impact strategy. Military questions like the following can help her work through consulting issues:

1. What supply-chain issues did the French face and how did it impact their decisions?

2. How did the cost of the war impact military strategy?

3. How were the local Viet soldiers mobilized and galvanized for actions?

4. How do you get troops to do the right thing at the right time when you cannot communicate with them twenty-four hours a day?

5. How did a vastly superior army lose to a tactically inferior and asset-light army?

6. Was the Vietnamese strategy to beat the French at Dien Bien Phu, and did they understand the psychological ripple effect of such a massive defeat?

7. How should tactics change over the course of a campaign?

8. When should a campaign show its hand?

At the end, I switch the discussion to lessons for business.

Relevance of Dien Bien Phu

We need to determine if entering the US is a strategically significant step for the bank to take. We must not take for granted that it is.

If the US is not, then we need to recommend they back away.

There is more than one path for the bank to achieve its goals, and the US market entry may not be the best choice for this banking client.

If the US market entry is the best option, then we need to think about how the bank, which theoretically is not as strong as the incumbents, can apply its weaknesses to win in the US market.

PAUSE & REFLECT

> What are the lessons that you take from the Battle of Dien Bien Phu?
> Why is strategy static in that most strategy engagements rarely consider how competitors will react?
> Who are LAB's competitors and how will they likely react?
> How will the Mexican government and populace react?

STRATEGY

25. THE COST OF CAPITAL DIFFERENTIAL IS A KEY ARBITER OF LAB'S OPTIONS.

Lower costs offer crucial advantages.

USING A LOWER WACC FOR A PRICING STRATEGY

Our hypothesis is that LAB should have a lower cost of capital than the current players in the US. This means it needs a formula for a lower average weighted cost of capital (WACC):

1. LAB has an implicit government guarantee on its balance sheet, and it is assumed the government will not allow LAB to default.

2. Private players in the US are either funded through retained earnings in the capital markets or via depository receipts. In aggregate, all will have a higher cost of capital attached to them.

3. US banks will probably be seen as lower risk, but the implicit assumption that the government owes and will bail out LAB may give it a lower risk weighting. This is something we need to check.

So, if LAB does have this advantage, and the US market is attractive, how do we use it?

1. Do we offer the best financial terms for customers?

2. Do we skim the market with a high price and, therefore, very high margin, but we offer very attractive support on mentoring and the like?

3. Do we offer a hybrid, with some segments getting the lowest financing costs and others getting higher financing costs?

If LAB's cost of capital is lower, will it use the same strategy as Toyota Finance & Leasing?

Because Toyota's financing arm is AAA-rated, the subsidiary can borrow money at the lowest rates and, therefore, offer customers better deals than financing rivals using a balance sheet with a lower-rated debt base.

This is a big reason Toyota has obliterated competitors in the low- and medium-price markets, where customers are sensitive to monthly payment plans that change by $20 to $50 a month.

Toyota's financing subsidiary can offer this advantage, and it is up to the operations people to implement it and implement it cost effectively so that the cost of implementation does not eat up the financing advantage.

LAB will need a superior system of risk management personnel and loan officers to limit defaults. If operators deploy the capital, borrowed at competitive rates, without carefully analyzing borrowers, defaults rise, the rating of the loan book drops, LAB's balance sheet deteriorates, and it will lose its implied AAA rating, or whatever rating the government backing LAB has.

So, you can see how strategy, financial strategy, and operations are linked?

If we assume LAB's major advantages are its cost of capital and risk management system, then:

1. Strategy determines where we deploy this advantage. (Our role.)
2. Operations ensures the business can prevent defaults, so that loans are repaid to keep the rating. (Partly our role insofar as

determining if entering the retail banking channel in the US will destroy capital.)

3. Financial strategy ensures LAB can use the strong credit ratings sustained above to move away from government recapitalizations, by borrowing money at very low rates in the capital markets. (Not our role.)

PAUSE & REFLECT

> Can you think of other examples where strategy, operations, and financing are so closely linked?

> What dangers exist if you recommend a strategy without considering the cash flow, income statement, and balance sheet impact?

> Why do so few business cases consider and calculate the balance sheet risk or the impact of a proposed strategy?

> Would you be a better consultant if you could speak to these risks?

WEEK 0: PLANNING

26. WOMEN SHOULD NOT BE PUNISHED FOR THEIR BEAUTY.

Even discussing beauty and dressing is wrong because we do not discuss these topics with men.

MENTORING WOMEN

Let's assume an engagement manager has what many would consider exotic features and is very beautiful. Let's assume she dresses well.

How do we advise her about sexism and the like without making her feel uncomfortable? And without making the partner uncomfortable?

The mere act of bringing it up could actually make her more self-conscious, especially if she has not thought about this issue before.

People simply assume they have done something wrong when they get advice, and we would like to avoid that.

We will go for an indirect strategy here: constantly emphasizing the values we have, how we treat clients, and how we respond to any slights of character.

In fact, by designating her as the team's number two, we can make the team and client give her the respect she deserves.

So, the strategy here is to actually deal with the circumstances regarding Nimisha versus making her do anything different.

If we were working on Wall Street, this would be an issue. In consulting, it is less of an issue.

However, we are working for a bank in a country that is generally less accommodating to female empowerment, especially darker-skinned females. So, some air cover is needed.

Like Marvin Bower said when he appointed McKinsey's first female engagement manager, do not ask the client if they are okay with the staffing, you show them it is okay.

We will follow the same strategy.

It goes without saying that Nimisha needs to rise to the occasion and demonstrate she respects the responsibility she is being given. Moreover, there should not be a double standard.

She will be held to the highest standards; we meet them on a consistent basis. There is often no recourse for failure in the eyes of a client.

That said, all the focus now goes to:

1. Onboarding the interns!
2. Onboarding the interns!!
3. Onboarding the interns!!!

The bigger the investment and thoroughness of the planning, the better the engagement will go. You can usually predict how well an engagement will go through two things:

1. The rigor and investment in recruiting
2. The rigor and investment in training and mentoring

As it stands, the original training agenda I prepared will be used.

STRATEGY

PAUSE & REFLECT

> If you are a female consultant, do you feel too much mentoring advice forces just YOU to change, versus your male co-workers?

> What would you change to make your firm more inclusive?

> What would you change about your behavior, language, and actions to be more accepting of other minorities?

WEEK 0: PLANNING

27. LACK OF CONFIDENCE FORCES POOR CHOICES IN IMAGE MANAGEMENT.

The urge to fit in can be damaging.

IMAGE MANAGEMENT

Strangely enough, many interns think overindulging in alcohol is a sign of being cool. If you like alcohol and it does not impact the engagement, that's fine. But it is best not to do it to fit in.

We see this a lot with many interns. They think drinking a lot is a sign of vigor and coolness.

We think it can be damaging if the culture of that team or, heaven forbid, the firm says it is acceptable.

I have seen interns and consultants say and do damaging things in this state. It is best not to show yourself when you're drunk, unless you are pretty sure it will help your career.

In other words: How does consuming alcohol help your career strategy?

If it does help your strategy, do it. If not, stay away.

This is not to say you should not do it but read the situation very carefully to ensure you are not hurting your image. We have been in situations where some office partners like drinking, and joining them means you fit in. On the other hand, tactfully not doing it does not alienate you.

Most times, interns do it because they do not know how to refuse indulging without alienating the team. In this case, practice how to politely socialize with the team, without drinking alcohol.

That is a skill worth learning. For instance, you could order a single glass of wine and sip it slowly over four hours. If you cannot drink at all for health, religious or some other reason, consider filling a wineglass with sparkling soda.

Never ever draw attention to your sobriety because all you are doing is showing you are the odd one out, which merely increases the pressure to conform. The trick is not to draw attention to your differences, but to find a way to practice your differences discreetly.

In the end, you should care about leaving your mark on the engagement, not about the alcohol you do or don't consume, or the size of the job offer you'll receive.

SIGNS OF PRIVILEGE

We find it distasteful when consultants abuse client privileges by ordering expensive meals because the client is paying, be it at client-sponsored dinners or on the engagement.

The rule is that we always order the "blue plate special," that is, a moderately priced dinner on the menu.

We serve the CEO at the pleasure of the shareholders, and no sane shareholder wants to see cash thrown away on dinners.

Does this mean we're cheap? Not at all. It is about managing the image of the firm.

Our fees will be set very high, and we will reward the interns through high salaries. But we should not be bleeding clients with elaborate dinners. The interns can buy their own lobster with their high salaries.

We do not encourage clients to take us out for expensive dinners. If we are paying, when we have a budget for this sort of entertaining, then it's fine.

STRATEGY

Image matters and these small issues count.

Showing the client you do not abuse their money is not the same as being cheap. You should be charging the client sufficiently large fees and expenses to treat the team well.

However, you should not throw around big spending in front of the client. The client needs to see that you treat their capital as if it were your own.

On the other hand, if you have low expenses and low fees, and you take the team to a budget diner for meals, then you are being cheap, and I'm not advocating that.

This advice is about how a premium firm with premium fees can demonstrate that they care.

How you look as you are conducting the engagement matters just as much as the quality of what you produce. It upsets and scares clients when consultants show that they:

1. Are disorganized.
2. Look stressed or scowl.
3. Seem close to collapsing in a meeting due to fatigue.
4. Have shaky hands due to lack of sleep or nervousness.

I insist that the team not only do a good job but also look the part. That means managing one's time to get sufficient sleep, eat well, drink sufficient liquids, and ask for help to limit time commitments.

Remember, no one wants to work for or with someone who exports anxiousness and stress. It can damage team dynamics and the confidence of the client.

ARROGANCE

You have probably heard a phrase like this during your engagement:

> "Don't worry. I'll get it to you about a day before it's needed, and I can do more than you asked."

Why say that? Why broadcast this? Why overpromise? How does it help you to do this?

If you deliver something earlier and of higher quality, then you will be rewarded. However, if you make a promise that you may end up not keeping, and if you fail to keep it, you lose credibility.

In other words, demonstrate your competency: Don't tell me what you'll do. Show me.

Albert suffers from this ego curse. He consistently overpromises and under delivers. If he did not overpromise, he would be fine. But sadly, he sets such high expectations that, even though his work is of the same quality as Peter's, Albert disappoints on these small things and that hurts his image.

Remember demonstrated competency? Don't tell me what you will do; just do it and show me the results.

PAUSE & REFLECT

> How has pressure to conform changed your behavior in the office?

> Has this helped you?

> How should you withdraw from an activity without judging your colleagues?

> How can you manage expectations better?

WEEK 0: PLANNING

28. READING AND INTERPRETING EXHIBITS IS A CRUCIAL SKILL.

Mastering this skill requires more than a role handling lots of data.

DATA SETS

I believe students must be drilled on the basics of reading large data sets. Some basic things everyone needs to ask when analyzing any data set should include:

1. What is the cause and effect?
2. Is the data cleaned for seasonality and other distorting factors?
3. How accurate is the insight, given the accuracy of the source data?
4. Why are we choosing these metrics to review the data? Are the metrics biased towards what we want to see?

Here is a classic example of **seasonality:**

Let's assume Amazon ships 37% more of your company's toys in December than in October. Will you give the managers of the toy division a big bonus?

We actually do not know if they should be fired, kept in their jobs or given a bonus until we test for a few things:

1. Did the market grow by 37% or more?

    If the market grew by 37%, then they simply rose with the tide.

    If the market grew by >37%, they lost market share.

    If the market grew by <37%, they gained market share.

2. Do toy sales usually rise in December?

   Do they rise by 37% on average?

   If yes to both, then we are seeing seasonal impact, and we need to strip this out to test the real growth in sales.

3. Did the sales gain in December pull forward purchases that would have been made at another time?

   In other words, did December sales rise at the expense of sales in the following months?

HOW DOES THIS APPLY TO LAB?

Launching a product in March and showing rapid uptake means little since the rate of loans approved naturally rises from spring to fall. This is the seasonal pattern we would expect.

We need to strip out this seasonality effect to see if the product is:

   a. Taking share or

   b. Growing the overall market.

This type of thinking is a game-changer.

FINAL PLANNING BEFORE INTERNS ARRIVE

A lot was accomplished this weekend:

1. All the pre-engagement reading of annual reports, newspaper articles, magazine clippings, and analyst reports.

2. Preparing the training pack and material for the onboarding.
3. Planning the agenda, initial questions for the focus interviews.

This week will fly by so quickly it might as well not be counted for any preparation.

1. The partner will sign off on the travel and hotel accommodation details for the team in about five minutes. Surprisingly, booking late allowed us to get some excellent rates at the hotels.
2. He will spend some time at the hotel going through the logistics for the internship onboarding.
3. He will also carry around my notebook to make sure any ideas or hypotheses I developed are not lost in the process.

Wednesday to Friday is pretty much completely out. We run the training all day and it will be tiring!

FOCUS INTERVIEWS

The team is splitting into two groups for the focus interviews. There should be two people in an interview: one to conduct the interview and one to take notes. If you have a transcriber to automatically take notes, then one person is fine. There is enormous value in taking along a younger consultant to teach them.

The good news is that all twenty-nine interview requests have been accepted. The bad news is that some interviewees want to do their interviews this Thursday and Friday.

Unfortunately, that can only happen if the interviews are after 6 p.m., since training is crucial, and I have no plans to cut it down. The success of the engagement will come down to the quality of the training.

SHADOW ENGAGEMENT TEMPLATES DONE AND DISTRIBUTED

We will begin the shadow studies of entrepreneurs very, very soon.

The template has been prepared, and we hope to have the final template done by this evening.

As the team conducts the shadow study, we want them to think about the following:

> How to (H2) Address segments with differing needs:

- Difference in finance requirements, needs, and products for rural versus urban customers or by type of business and industry.
- Types of entities financed by El Toro.

> H2 Address LAB's target segments currently not addressed by existing channels:

- Types of segments or industries not being addressed by El Toro.
- Any opportunities or gaps, specific mentorship and after-care needs not being met.

> H2 Build channel advocacy for LAB's products through existing channels:

- Awareness by El Toro employees of other products and services not being offered.
- Benefits of and concerns about current LAB products.

> H2 Take advantage of or contribute to the BEE Financial Charter:

- Any opportunities or activities being undertaken with other institutions.

- Involvement with larger banks or other government institutions.

H2 Coordinate LAB's position and activities with other government departments and NGOs:

- Any opportunities or activities being undertaken with other institutions.
- Involvement with larger banks or other government institutions.

H2 Manage expectations of stakeholders reentering the DFI market:

- Benefits, concerns, questions, or other comments about LAB initiatives or press exposure.
- Probe for opportunities or space for new players to enter.

H2 Grow the LAB loan book on a sustainable basis:

- Commt rates charged, and terms and conditions.
- Loan size and people support and number of employees.
- Interest rates charged, and terms and conditions.

The template itself, **Exhibit 13,** is very simple. It is more useful to collect simple data. Great insights don't often come from complex data collection. They are generated from carefully thinking about the meaning of the basic data collected.

This template is such an example. It is one of the most basic data collection sheets we could have developed, but it could yield great insights. In just about every engagement, the client has usually seen the data before.

However, we present and interpret the data in a different way. This is the value we bring.

WEEK 0: PLANNING

EXHIBIT 13: Shadow study template

Time and Activity Sheet

FUNCTION/OPERATION PERFORMED: BAD DEBTS COLLECTION /DEBTOR MANAGEMENT. OBSERVER: NIMISHA

Time	Activity description	Comments	Key Take-out
11:30 to 11:49 (19 mins)	Called customer X to follow up on overdue payment. Made four calls before reaching right person. Updated debtors' system with reason code and new expected payment date.	Payment overdue by three days. Sally says this is a typical customer. Most people who don't pay do so for silly reasons, e.g., moved business premises. On average, 34 calls made per day.	Customers frequently forget to pay and need to be reminded. Follow-up calls required in 10% of cases.
11:50 to 12:00 (10 mins)	etc	etc	etc
12:01 to 13:10 (9 mins)	etc	etc	etc
13:11 to 14:05 (54 mins)	etc	etc	etc

The team will fan out and conduct entrepreneur shadow studies in seven states:

1. New York (control)
2. California
3. Arizona
4. Nevada
5. New Mexico
6. Texas
7. Florida
8. Later, we will add three more southern states in the engagement.

STRATEGY

PAUSE & REFLECT

- Does your firm do this level of planning and preparation before an engagement?
- How would you improve your pre-engagement planning?
- Should the client be billed for this time?
- How should your firm include and explain this additional cost to the client?

WEEK 0: PLANNING

STRATEGY

29. HAVING A RELIABLE INSIDE SOURCE AT THE CLIENT IS A VALUABLE ASSET.

Without them, you are basically parachuting a team in with little knowledge of what to expect.

OUR GUIDE

The partner will have a late breakfast at Starbucks with the newest member of our team. He is a 63-year-old veteran development finance expert whom Guillermo wanted to be on the team to help us navigate the issues and personalities in the sector.

We are looking forward to meeting him. So far, we've heard high praise for his skills, and we think he could add tremendous value in helping us analyze the feedback we receive.

At 63, I hope he will be able to manage the pace of the engagement. I need to make a mental note to ensure we don't walk between all of our interviews.

The key thing for Andreas, the expert, is whether he is going to be a specialist due to his past knowledge, his thinking skills, or a combination of both. I would prefer the third, the hybrid.

We would want his feedback on:

- The shadow-engagement questionnaire
- Focus interview questions (at this stage we have just a rough draft)
- Proposed case studies
- Proposed engagement structure

My initial hypotheses (which the team is bound to revise once they take ownership of them)

LAB'S TRUE PROBLEMS

Andreas is a very knowledgeable and forthright person, maybe too forthright. He shared some clues about the engagement. We have already inferred some of the information from the data and hypothesized it ourselves. Nonetheless, here it is:

1. The bank's performance has not been great in the last few years. In fact, since its founding, the bank has failed to meet its expectations on creating jobs and economic sustainability.

2. The two main investors, the government and a private fund, are chomping at the bit to see better results.

3. The government brought in the private investor to inject better management and lending practices. It has not worked so well.

4. The bank has failed to create sufficient jobs and is struggling to find recipients for its entrepreneurial financial products.

5. The returns have been very low and while the audited statements are positive, if you read between the lines, LAB is not earning its cost of capital. (We concur with this from reading the annual reports, but we still need to prove it).

6. The bank is not growing. Growth has stalled, and it has a ton of cash on its balance sheet that is not invested in anything meaningful.

7. The US market-entry plan is a forced move by the CEO to show he is trying something bold to turn the company around.

STRATEGY

This is not forced by the shareholders but by members of the management team, who feel they need something dramatic to turn the business around.

8. The analyses supporting the US market-entry decision are not correct, nor does Andreas feel the internal strategy team is approaching this in the right way.

9. The bank could destroy up to $1 billion in capital if this entry is wrong for LAB, or if it is right but fails.

10. The private banks who sell LAB's products hate working with LAB and consistently allow the credit guarantees to be called up since they allow the loans to default.

Andreas believes the banks will retaliate if the client moves from the wholesaler to retailer model. Andreas believes it is only a matter of time before there is a massive leadership change and a change to the overall strategy.

Good food for thought. This does not change much for us though.

That said, this engagement could easily morph from a market-entry strategy to a full corporate strategy.

We think LAB will be using the following strategy and argument with the US government to get a banking license, with LAB adding in the numbers once they have them:

1. We, LAB, will invest $TK million, which will create, among entrepreneurs, TK000 new jobs and $TK million in new revenue.

2. Moreover, our superior process and risk management will lead to reduced inefficiencies of TK% for entrepreneurs, which leads to that saved time being spent on productive activity like

increasing sales by $TK million across a portfolio of TK million borrowers.

3. This translates to a TK% growth in US GDP and a TK% increase in tax revenue.

4. We feel that is a worthy return for a banking license.

That is the high-level business case thinking. Of course, LAB will have to meet all the capital, risk management and compliance requirements as well.

The subtle point is that the US can better leverage the emigrants within its borders to give them a path to the middle class and simultaneously lift the US economy.

The government does not have many other choices. Banks will not serve this segment, and without a path to create wealth, many will be dependent on government assistance for a large chunk of their lives. Moreover, the children of this segment, as well as grandchildren and beyond, would contribute on average less in terms of taxes or productivity if this segment is struggling financially.

That is not a thrilling proposition for anyone. Especially those trapped in low-income jobs.

The crucial point LAB is making is that they are not asking for US government help. They will be deploying capital from a foreign government.

Most current initiatives to help low-income entrepreneurs rely on some kind of assistance from the US government.

PAUSE & REFLECT

> Is the direction of the engagement shifting from the original issues?
> Is this necessary, a mistake, or scope creep?
> How should we manage this shift with the client?
> How would you use hypotheses that are being constantly refined to advance an engagement?
> Why do we invest so much in the planning phase?

WEEK 0: PLANNING

30. THE TEAM IS STRUCTURED TO START LIKE A GREYHOUND, SLOW DOWN A LITTLE, AND END ON A HIGH.

The pace of insights you want should determine the staffing roles.

FOUR X 100-METER PRINCIPLES

As we've mentioned a few times, the pace at which we run this engagement will be frightening if you are not accustomed to it, or not accustomed to communicating in that mode.

I need to think about how to ensure the consultants do things that allow them to keep up the momentum. These will help:

- Not skipping breakfast
- Remaining hydrated
- Eating well
- Resting well
- Planning well
- Not allowing anxiousness to show
- Sleeping on time

These things will determine if the interns can keep up. My biggest worry is that one of the consultants will decide that he or she cannot keep up, will stop caring, and will just go through the motions. Though we have a contingency plan for that, it is far better to avoid the contingency plan.

STREAMS

We are going to structure the engagement as follows:

1. Academic Advisers – three academic advisers from Yale, Harvard, and Oxford will advise on the validity of our approach.

2. Partner responsible for the strategy.

3. Nimisha – Engagement manager responsible for the engagement coordination and strategy.

4. Peter – Best practices analyses led by a market analysis, case study analyses, and day-in-the-life-of studies.

5. Albert – Value analyses to test the economics of entering the US market via a retail branch network.

This is where the "4 x 100 meter" relay thinking comes in.

1. Albert will need to complete the top-down analyses to point out the likely issues at the client.

2. Peter will have to set things off with a very effective set of guidelines, priorities, and insights from the interviews and case studies, to guide the economic modelling and assumptions we can use.

3. Albert needs to present the detailed economics of market entry.

5. Nimisha and I are working intimately with the rest of the team and Andreas, and will need to draw together all the insights. We will anchor the team.

Note how important the anchor leg will be. That is why Nimisha will have general accountability throughout the engagement but no deliverable responsibility until the last four weeks. I want her to know everything that is happening, but to be ready to really push in the last few weeks to bring everything together.

Basically, I do not want her to suffer from burnout coming into the last four weeks. She needs to be at her best during this time.

The anchor on the team is the most crucial role. It usually goes to the most capable and mature team member.

On the flip side, Albert and Peter will have completed most of their work by Weeks 7 and 8 so they are able to assist heavily as we come into the final stretch. We hope Albert might find his second wind from week 9 to help us tease out the key economic insights.

WEEK 0: PLANNING

PAUSE & REFLECT

> Do you think the pace of the insights required should be taken into consideration when staffing an engagement?

> How do you manage your tasks on an engagement running at this pace?

> Is it fair to the team for the partner and engagement manager to run an engagement at this pace?

STRATEGY

31. CASE STUDIES ADD VALUE IF YOU ARE CLEAR ABOUT THEIR PURPOSE.

Most case studies are neat, unverified, and unhelpful summaries of media articles and annual reports.

OBJECTIVE FUNCTION

It will be crucial to set a clear objective function in this engagement and use that to derive the sub-questions.

If we do not do so, we run the risk of examining interesting but unnecessary questions.

We need to be brutally efficient about being focused on maximizing the objective function, which at this stage appears to be:

> Is entering the US market via a retail distribution network the best means for LAB to meet its mandate in the short, medium and long term?

We have noticed that the auditor's notes have not been published in their entirety in the annual report. LAB did not submit a copy to us. That is usually a warning sign. Albert will need to meet the auditors to see the original notes. We need to know what they saw.

SCOPE VS. DEPTH

This will not be a broad engagement. We will keep the scope tight.

It will rather be a sweeping analysis around a tight topic. We will go deep on a narrow scope of work.

We will not be studying every irrelevant fact related to development finance and microfinance or the unbanked in the US. This is a mistake most consultants will make.

We only need to analyze enough to answer the problem statement above.

SETTING UP THE CASE STUDIES

Andreas and the partner had a late discussion last night about some changes to the case study list.

We decided to add an Indonesian bank to the list of initial case studies. In fact, that will be the first case study with which we open the analyses.

Why? Because:

> Indonesia is a large source of immigrants to the US.

> Indonesian immigrants would be familiar with LAB's operations.

> If it's possible, LAB could tailor some of its products around the case study model.

The Indonesian basic economy in many ways mirrors the underground economy in the US border states. There are vast differences, of course, but some crucial similarities include:

> A low level of regional security (these are immigrants in the US who may face deportation and sometimes lack access to basic rights).

> Due to the above, there's a lack of reliable recourse to contract disputes.

> A weak banking system (for immigrants).

> No IMF oversight (the IMF does not have state oversight in the US).

Andreas will arrange for us to speak to the CEO and the head of strategy and planning at the bank so we at least know the data can be corroborated if we chose to do the detailed case study of the bank.

EARLY THOUGHTS FOR THE CASE STUDIES

I would want Peter to think about the major sub-questions that drive the main question in the engagement, and he should try to answer them through his case study analyses. These issues include:

How important are ownership, management, and governance issues and incentives in the survival of small businesses?

> How do successful development finance banks balance costly job creation with the need to make profits?
>
> Should LAB serve the entire US low-income market, just some states, some segments, or even some ethnic groups?
>
> How important is it for the bank to control the distribution channel to increase loan disbursements?
>
> What risk management skills will be needed in a retail roll versus a wholesale roll?
>
> How can LAB minimize risk at the institutional balance sheet level?
>
> What interest should the bank charge?
>
> How important is sustainability to LAB?
>
> Does the bank have incompatible goals?

US-SPECIFIC QUESTIONS

He also needs to consider questions to understand the US market, such as:

> Are the interest rates charged from unregulated brokers so high that they are causing borrowers to default?
>
> What happens if the borrower cannot repay the loan: Are the assets seized, are his knees capped or both?
>
> If a Yale kid launches a start-up and fails, he can simply try again. What are the consequences when immigrant entrepreneurs fail?
>
> How is cash saved?
>
> How much time and additional costs go into settling payments without a proper banking card or bank account?
>
> How does the threat of deportation drive behavior that hurts the business? (This might include using expensive money transfer programs if you do not have the documents to open a bank account).
>
> What are the time savings, cost savings (if any), and investment required to correct these problems?

I am not sure we will answer all of this, since it is not necessary to our objective function, but it would be useful to determine which are necessary to answer.

PAUSE & REFLECT

> Have you found case studies to be useful during strategy engagements?
> What are the hallmarks of a good case study?
> What is the ideal length, in pages, of a case study?
> How do you prove a contention in your case study?

STRATEGY

32. THE ENGAGEMENT OFFICE SHOULD BE A SAFE ZONE, CLOSED OFF FROM THE CLIENT.

Given the high pressures involved, the interns need a space where they feel normal.

SAFE ZONES

Guillermo likes the way we are managing things and wants to be more involved. He feels sitting in the engagement room with us will help him and us.

Unfortunately, this is not a great idea since engagements are messy and we need the space to be messy. Moreover, we report to the CEO and need to discuss many things before we produce nice, neat answers. The discussions may not be pretty, but they lead to the right answers.

And this is one of the problems with strategy in general. Many assume the answers jump out of the analyses. They do not. They slowly develop as a series of conversations revolving around the analyses.

In fact, this is why we are releasing this book in such an unorthodox format versus other books on strategy and management. We believe you must see the messiness to understand how a strategy engagement develops. Other books want to just show you the end result.

I explained this to Guillermo. He understood since he was a McKinsey associate. This is the benefit of an ex-consulting client. They understand the truth and accept it.

STRATEGY

ANDREAS'S SUGGESTION ON PROJECTING POWER

Andreas advised us that we need to be very aggressive and not allow the other consultants to hijack the engagement. He suggested being very tough in meetings and pushing back.

I think that is wrong.

If we do our work diligently, communicate well, and our logic is sound, the work will speak for itself. We do not need to project power.

In fact, I find that consultants at weaker firms are the worst at belittling competitors, aggressively controlling engagements, and strong-arming other firms. We will be intellectually aggressive for sure, but we will deploy that with a velvet touch.

We do not need to play games. Those who have influence and power do not need to do anything. We serve at the pleasure of the CEO, on behalf of the shareholders, and we just need to do our job. Everything will take care of itself. With good intentions and brilliant thinking come great rewards.

Only those who lack power need to overtly attempt to project power.

In fact, the Ranatunga Doctrine is about a rapid buildup of insights, but it is done in a very polite manner. We need to focus on the engagement and not get distracted by petty turf wars.

Displacing the other consultants and pleasing the client are mutually exclusive goals. We should avoid the trap of thinking they are one and the same.

Unsurprisingly, we are also routinely asked how our firm is better than another firm?

Another firm is the dominant firm at this client, so it surprises and intrigues many to see us doing this work.

The partner does not answer this question, and the team is trained not to answer this question. We do not even mention other firms by name. We keep the narrative on the work.

This morning, when asked this question, we responded by saying, "I am sure all other firms are very good at what they do, but I am not an expert to comment on them. I would rather discuss this engagement and demonstrate how we are going to solve the problem. Would you like us to take you through our thinking?"

This throws off the person asking the question because they have historically received a monologue when they asked other firms this question.

Note, we did not mention the names of the other firms in my response. Why advertise for them? They don't exist in my mind.

Moreover, focusing clients on our thinking is another way of displaying demonstrated competency. We do not tell the client why we are better. We show the client.

We do not talk about why we are better, but we hope to demonstrate this through our work.

And if our work is not good, we will take the criticism and improve.

The team is trained not to belittle or ridicule competitors. We take them very, very seriously. Remember Dien Bien Phu and the Battle of Stalingrad? Try not to underestimate your competitors. You should respect them and honor them but ensure that your values and way of approaching clients is a superior system that will triumph over the long term.

We do not believe we are better.

We do, however, believe that as an organization we exist solely to place our clients' interests first and leave them better off than when we arrived. Very few organizations can say that about themselves.

We are not a business. We are a philosophy practiced by professionals who view ethical business leadership as the highest calling. This is enshrined in our values and will likely change.

Yes, we will initially be weak in some areas, lack some skills, but I trust that our values, culture, systems, and processes will allow us to do a better job by the end of the engagement.

They have not failed us before.

The onboarding continuously drills this into the interns. Our values, culture, philosophy, and more are superior.

PAUSE & REFLECT

> How can you deploy this approach to protect your firm's reputation?

> How would you manage a situation where a client is unwilling to give your team their own space?

> How would you explain to the client the benefit of allocating this space?

STRATEGY

33. CONSULTING TEAMS SHOULD BE TRAINED TO MANAGE ENGAGEMENTS FOR TIMES WHEN THINGS GO WRONG.

Training only for the best conditions is not useful.

DISASTER DRILLS

This is a very key tactic that we deploy in our training.

Most firms have a pretty big flaw in their training. They show you best practice in a sterile setting, which does not replicate a real client situation. They spend 95% of the time talking about how to produce good slides, analyses and output, and maybe drop in a vague mention of how to handle problems.

We adapt our training substantially such that 50% of the training is focused on what to do when things do not go according to plan. There are enormous benefits to this approach:

1. Things go wrong in engagements all the time and by openly discussing this and having a game plan for it, the team feels comfortable should anything happen.

    They do not delay in bringing it up nor do they try to cover up problems. The approach builds trust.

2. It builds morale. When things go wrong on an engagement, it damages morale and causes members to withdraw.

    With this approach, members are expecting trouble, know the partners are expecting trouble, and are drilled in knowing how to respond.

3. We do not give up at the end of an engagement. In fact, we really turn up the pace with about 25% of the time to go. Typically, things go wrong near the end when fatigue sets in.

   Knowing we have tools, techniques, and processes to manage this situation allows the team to really push harder at the end.

Most of Thursday and Friday will be simulations to show the team how to respond to problems that could include:

Slides are not done on time.

Incorrect data is submitted.

The client is not submitting data on time.

The modelling is incorrect.

The analyses are not proving our hypotheses or cannot be done.

A deliverable cannot be met in the time available.

There are errors in the analyses and the client is upset.

Remember we are using the Ranatunga Doctrine, which calls for this massive push from hour one, but this tactic allows us to really push at the end of the engagement when things go a little off, as they tend to.

Sir Alex Ferguson actually trained Manchester United in intensive drills on what to do when they were two goals down with fifteen minutes remaining.

We follow the same tactic. We do not merely hope for everything to work. We have detailed protocols for when things do go wrong.

PAUSE & REFLECT

> What has happened to you on an engagement where things went wrong, and you were not trained to manage the situation?

> How did you rectify the problem?

> Have you documented that lesson for your colleagues?

> Does your firm only discuss well-managed engagements?

> How can you discuss the lessons for a poorly managed engagement without offending any of the team members involved?

STRATEGY

34. INTERNS ARE FUTURE CEOS AND SHOULD BE TREATED AS SUCH.

An internship should be designed to teach interns versus wringing them out.

PUT THE TEAM FIRST

Most consulting firms will basically kill their interns to ensure the engagement is done to the highest standards. In fact, a partner or manager could get fired if the engagement completed with the interns is a disaster.

We take a long-term view. We are building the firm for the long-term and burning out interns to please a client is a myopic mindset. What does it actually accomplish if you deliver the engagement with a burnt-out team? Consider this scenario:

> The engagement is a success and maybe this leads to more work.
>
> Yet the interns end up hating consulting.
>
> They suffer from burnout.
>
> They hate us, the firm that hired them.
>
> So we end up with more work and no one to deliver it.
>
> There is a need for balance.

So, in these situations, the partner will carry much of the weight, constantly pushing the interns forward to be better than they were before they started. We cannot, however, reasonably expect an intern to perform as well as an associate with two years of consulting experience.

If you take care of the person, the person takes care of the team, and if the team feels taken care off, they take care of the firm, and by doing so the client always benefits.

The firm benefits in the long term.

Language also matters here. We ask team members not to say "I" for any reason. It is always "we." This is how we instill this practice:

> **Peter:** When I complete the first case study...
>
> **Partner:** Not "I." It's always "we."
>
> **Peter:** Is that not misleading?
>
> **Partner:** We are not discussing ownership. You are speaking for the team. And when it comes to the reviews, I know who did the work.
>
> **Peter:** It's still misleading.
>
> **Partner:** No. It's only misleading if you worry about credit. You can take ownership for the case study, but I am interested in the insight. So, I can give you credit for doing the case study, but that credit is worth zero. I am interested in what you have to say about the case study.
>
> **Peter:** So, ownership is not about effort?
>
> **Partner:** Bingo. Own the insight. And you will own the insight when you tell me the insight. But there is no credit for telling me you did a case study lacking an insight.

The key to achieving this is to hire young people as interns before they have picked up the corporate culture of another firm. And then you slowly develop and train them to think in our way.

Consulting firms with weaker cultures and a deep profit focus tend to bring in senior and experienced people with, sometimes, horrendous values just so they can deliver the current engagement well. But they will have basically poisoned the firm with their values in the process.

This is why we rarely allow ex-consultants of any firm to serve on our engagements. We want to groom interns to be future leaders within our firm. Yes, they will make mistakes, but that is part of the short-term price of building a long-term culture.

This is another lesson from Sir Alex Ferguson, who brought in many youngsters and allowed them to suffer several defeats while they were groomed in the way of Manchester United.

You cannot and should not replace people when they struggle, provided they have the raw skills, right values, want to learn, have tried their best, and somehow got to the finish line. Good consultants all struggle at first. Even partners struggle.

STRATEGY

PAUSE & REFLECT

> Do you feel that your firm takes the long-term view when developing consultants?

> What could they change to take a long-term view?

> What can you do on Monday morning at 8 a.m. to take control of your career development?

WEEK 0: PLANNING

35. GOOD TRAINING MUST ADJUST AS THE MOOD AND ENERGY LEVELS OF THE PARTICIPANTS CHANGE.

Never ever trust a training program with a set agenda.

TOO AMBITIOUS

I think the training may have been a little too ambitious.

One key assumption made was that the interns watched, read, and understood all the preparation material from the technology corporate strategy. That turned out to be false.

Rather than trying to cover everything, I have prepared a contingency plan with a reduced agenda in the event this happened.

I am going to have to focus on values, ethics, and core skills like structuring engagements, developing hypotheses, storyboards and the like.

Does this worry me? Not in the least. This happens all the time.

We do not win awards for covering all the material in the training since the objective of the training is to have trained consultants. That means adjusting the training as the retention rate of the interns changes.

CRITICAL DOES NOT EQUAL INTELLIGENT.

Interns must not assume they are being intelligent if they are critical. The big picture is more meaningful than whether every line is correct.

Granted, there are some typos in the material, BUT accuracy is not the same as precision.

Being critical is the same as being precise but being precisely correct about the wrong issues still means you will fail.

In corporate strategy, we are setting in motion plans that will be rolled out over two to five years.

We cannot wait to get every number correct.

That is why there are assumptions and principles.

WAS THE TRAINING SUCCESSFUL?

Yes, by the standards every firm uses. Consulting firms do not expect much from the internal training for interns. At best, they expect the interns to know the terminology and the location of key people and resources, and they should basically be able to pull off looking like a consultant.

We have felt that was an atrocious target, even when we led training at the firm.

We wanted this training to teach the interns.

How did we plan that?

Our strategy was to use well-known examples in the media to explain key strategy and economic concepts. However, it soon became apparent that since we wanted the interns to have a much more practical knowledge of corporate strategy, using general examples was not going to work.

They struggled to extract the key concept from the general example and then to apply that concept to the client.

So, from around 11a.m. on the first day, we changed the examples to only examples from the engagement. This means that, from just before lunch, we have been going through really detailed discussions of the economics of development finance, microfinance, entrepreneurial finance, retail banking, and more as we taught them about hypotheses and so on.

The training concepts were pitched perfectly, but in the time, we had, it made no sense to use examples from outside the sector.

At least the core training material is working.

The good news is this means we are in some ways starting the engagement earlier because the discussions we are having now, I had planned for Monday.

And seeing how much time is needed to explain the concepts, I am glad this happened.

STAMINA

We are deploying the Ranatunga Doctrine, which calls for this blitzkrieg of a start to the engagement.

But there is a problem here. That doctrine calls for a fit team with mental and physical stamina.

For context, remember that twenty-nine focus interviews will be done in just the first week. That is fifteen per team and about four a day. At about one and a half hours per interview, plus traveling and transcribing, that is a hectic pace.

We will also do shadow studies and other work, after spending all Monday just planning.

Why does this worry me?

We could see the team getting tired just after lunch.

We want to attribute this to travel, jet lag, and possibly the partner's boring style, but we feel that the pace is going to be a problem.

We somewhat expected this and have planned to be with the team throughout the engagement so we can guide them well and support them anyone is struggling to keep up.

But it does worry us. If you see the level of insight we are planning to bring to the table, you will realize how much needs to be done in terms of input to generate that insight.

IMPORTANCE OF AN OBJECTIVE FUNCTION

As we conduct the training, the interns refer to earlier studies done by the World Bank, IMF, Bain, and others who include analyses that we are not doing.

This is the way most consultants work; they simply try to be comprehensive in their analyses.

We are trying to solve a key question for this client—maximize an objective function.

Only analyses that directly allow us to answer that question must be done. Everything else should be ignored.

The whole approach from objective function to hypotheses and storyboarding is about linking everything back to the objective function.

Yes, the World Bank did different analyses, but they quite possibly were answering a different question.

The same for Bain.

Moreover, we should not assume the other studies were any good. They may have been the best studies, but we really don't know the problem statement they were trying to find a solution for. Not all development finance studies are answering the same question.

The "why" is more important than the "what."

Even if you did the best market segmentation engagement ever completed by an associate or intern, which won accolades and the client loved, you would be penalized if you could not answer these questions:

> Why have we done this engagement?

> How does the market segmentation help us maximize this objective function?

> What will we do with the findings from the market segmentation engagement?

> Was there an easier way to do this?

The objective function drives everything. This is the problem with consultants from smaller firms and interns in general. They worry about the analyses done at McKinsey, BCG, or Bain. What another firm did should not matter.

They should worry more about learning how we determine which analyses should be done.

KNOW WHAT IS AT STAKE

On these types of engagements, where we can make a material sociological-economic impact, the team naturally wants to do well.

They want to help people.

That said, it is nonetheless vital to remember who the client is, and our job is to ensure the client is successful over the long term.

To get the interns to really understand the damaging impact of a bad recommendation, the partner presents an Eastern European case study of a prior engagement I led, with photos and other documentation.

In this engagement, the client had two options to build a steel mill and only one town could obtain the investment.

Using before and after photos, we showed them what happens to the town that did not receive the investment:

1. Unemployment surged to 55%.
2. Thousands left for better work in London, Warsaw, Moscow, and elsewhere.
3. Crime spiked as the policing budget fell.
4. Education levels dropped, and fewer children went to university.
5. It had a generational impact since the children of their children had diminished opportunities.

To make them understand the emotional trauma, we showed actual photos of a beautiful young child and her family as her town atrophied over the years. We showed them the limited choices she had and how she ended up as a teenager.

The point is this: Economics is about scarcity and, in a manner of speaking, management consultants often serve in the role of advisers to arbiters and judges of where to allocate the capital.

Someone will typically lose in the short term when capital is not allocated to them, and it is painful for the short-term loser to adjust. Sometimes, though, they do not adjust. Sometimes, they do not improve. Sometimes, they live the same lifestyle as their parents, and their children and grandchildren live the same way.

They do not experience economic mobility.

When possible, we need to make sure the right recipients get the capital.

This is a key session to drive home the importance of why we do what we do.

WEEK 0: PLANNING

PAUSE & REFLECT

> How do you keep the importance of what you are doing in the back of your mind at all times?

> How can your firm improve its training?

> What can you do to contribute to your firm's training?

> Does your firm financially reward the best trainers, and if not, how does this impact the quality of the training?

STRATEGY

36. IT IS A GOOD SIGN TO BE GENUINELY EXCITED THE DAY BEFORE A MAJOR ENGAGEMENT BEGINS.

The day you stop being excited is the day to quit.

PREPARATION

First sleep in forty-three hours.

The partner suffers from insomnia and can work long stretches without sleep.

His work suffers from about 6 a.m. to 9 a.m., but then he shifts back to normal and can see no impact.

Most of the updates have been about the process we have followed for training.

We are now working on the second draft of the focus interview questions and come Monday of next week, the posts will shift to strategy, economics, corporate finance, and retail banking, with a microfinance twist.

I want to start the focus interviews at 12 p.m. ET on Tuesday, which means all of the team's core planning must be done by this time. All of the following must be done:

- Charters
- Engagement logic
- Timelines
- Issue maps (very useful)

STRATEGY

- First draft of the storyboards
- First cut of the hypotheses
- First cut of the analyses
- First cut of the data needs

The value-analyses stream also needs to have the profit drivers and levers, and the plan for the top-down financial analyses, which should be completed in a twenty-four-hour sprint.

Many people are shocked when they read that the top-down financial analyses of even a multibillion-dollar market-capitalization conglomerate should be completed in twenty-four hours.

In our other books[31,32] and this study video program[33], we explain how and why to do this, and we provide guidelines.

Suffice it to say, this is easy to do once you know how to do it. And this is not the economic modelling work. That comes later. Financial modelling and financial analyses are different.

So, Monday is a big day. That said, we expect the team to use the weekend to also do this work. We need the work done since the analyses will determine the questions, we need to ask in the focus interviews.

That must be done on Monday, and the final draft of the focus interviews must be ready Monday night, with everything printed and ready to go on Tuesday.

---

[31] Safarova, Kris, *The Strategy Journal*, https://amzn.to/2QGft9d

[32] Safarova, Kris, *Succeeding as a Management Consultant*, 2nd ed., https://amzn.to/3a3atTn

[33] https://www.strategytraining.com/market-entry-strategy-program

ROUGH LAYOUT OF THE FOCUS INTERVIEW

We will add and remove things as informed by the data the team needs, which is informed by the team's hypotheses to be tested, which is informed by the branches of the decision tree the team prioritized, which is informed by the objective function of the case.

That said, having built all of that in my head, this is what I roughly developed as the sections:

> Market structure
>
> Market economics
>
> LAB's effectiveness
>
> Other items

As you can see, this is a very broad focus interview. It is helping us use industry experts to weed out issues that we will then need to prioritize. We must then determine whether they are the real problem and solution, and worthy of further analysis.

SHADOW STUDIES VS. FOCUS INTERVIEWS

Focus interviews are detailed questionnaires we have for experts, clients of LAB, and players in the value chain.

Shadow studies are where we spend a day following around entrepreneurs to gain an understanding of their lives.

We will do two types of shadow studies:

1. one type for entrepreneurs, and
2. another type for the distribution finance intermediaries (DFIs) in the US who borrow from LAB to lend to the entrepreneurs.

STRATEGY

That is a lot to do in the first two weeks.

In addition, the value analysis stream must complete the top-down basic financial analyses of LAB, while the markets stream must start the case studies and map the market structure.

It's going to be epic.

PAUSE & REFLECT

> What does your first day on an engagement typically look like?
> How can you be more productive?
> Why do we expect the consultants to do so much over just one day?
> What tools and training must you have to operate as productively as this team?

STRATEGY

37. THE ABILITY TO LEAVE YOUR EGO AT THE DOOR WILL MAKE YOU A GREAT CONSULTANT.

There is no excuse for belittling a client.

VALUE-BASED ADVANTAGE

One area we really emphasize and really excel at is knowing how to read people and work with them.

At the firm, the partner was a trouble shooter. His job was to go into very tough situations where the senior client was generally very unhappy and turn around the engagement and relationship.

It is crucial that the team be professional and focused, without coming across as arrogant and defensive.

This takes some skill, but it can be learned.

Any hostile client relationship can be turned into a productive partnership if you are sincere, open and willing to listen.

There are a few things for which you cannot prepare:

The client insults your gender.

The client insults your ethnicity.

The client openly ridicules you.

The client calls you an epithet. An actual client once called me a "Doberman," but I am going to believe it was meant as a compliment.

In such situations, which can be serious, you need to let the partner handle it with the senior client. These are serious breaches of professionalism that should not happen.

Junior members tend to unnecessarily escalate these situations and given the stature of the firm and team, who report straight to the CEO, this will rarely happen.

If it does happen, it is probably coming from someone who is unhappy with the engagement rather than being unhappy with the team member himself.

I tend to ignore these comments, stay professional, and focus on the results. That actually embarrasses the person delivering the insult because they notice they cannot get a reaction.

If you strike back at the client, it is a far worse issue.

A RIVAL CONSULTING FIRM RESPONDS

A rival firm has offered to do the retail market-entry engagement for free. That is not surprising.

In fact, I am surprised it took them so long to respond.

Any major firm would react if a boutique, even one set up by their own alums, was awarded work with the CEO of a major client.

But we are different, and this firm is not aware of that:

1. We do not bid for work nor do we respond to requests for proposals (RFPs). We must be invited to the engagement on a sole sourced bid. So, we do not bid for this work and have nothing to prove.

The client knows we will literally bleed before we let them fail. Our reputation precedes our determination, and our capabilities are well known. The other firm is not aware we did not bid for the work.

2. We actually did not want the work at first. We teach strategy and are an investment firm. We only take on engagements to further those two ends.

   We felt it was not something we could do, given the limited time we have and all the issues at the client. Initially, we suggested the other firm do the work.

   Therefore, the client is convinced our reasons for doing the work are very sincere. In fact, we offered to check the work for free and encouraged the client to get another firm since we had no time. The client knows we are not just doing this for the money.

3. This comes back to an earlier article[34] the partner wrote. When you have financial freedom, you can design an engagement that you care about. It is not about the money.

   You can pick and choose assignments that matter to you personally, and when clients know you care about something, it's unlikely they will let you go, no matter who offers to do it for free.

In fact, implying work can be done for free is slightly demeaning to the client and their customers. This work has value. Why do it for free?

---

[34] "Career Lessons From McKinsey's Hypothetical Death," https://www.firmsconsulting.com/quarterly/career-lessons-mckinseys-hypothetical-death/

Nothing is free. This means that firm has charged so much for other work at the client that they can absorb these costs. Or it means they don't expect this study to be that intensive and will probably lightly staff it. Or they will be biased to force a bigger engagement afterwards to make up for costs of doing this work for free.

No interpretation presents this firm in the best light.

Tomorrow is the final day of the training, and it is a good day for three reasons:

1. We will conduct extensive drills to make sure the team knows exactly what to do when something goes wrong.
2. We will unseal most of the engagement data so the team can dive into it.
3. The client, Guillermo, will attend to discuss some of the broad issues facing LAB.

We may add a module on moving from hypotheses to analyses since we think the team is a little weak at this.

PAUSE & REFLECT

> How have you responded to insults from a client?
> Did you get the outcome you sought?
> How do you manage perceived insults that are driven by cultural differences?
> How do you learn strategy if most organizations consult on strategy, but don't teach strategy?

STRATEGY

38. FORGET EVERYTHING A FIRM CLAIMS TO BE. THEY ARE WHO THEY HIRE AND WHAT THEY REWARD.

Values are built one employee at a time and diluted one acquisition and one wrong hire at a time.

AVOIDING CONSULTANTS

When hiring, we aim to bring in people who have incredible problem-solving skills, great initiative, and incredible ethics.

For the applicants who made it to the final rounds to join the engagement, this will surprise you to know:

> We had an MBA graduate who had worked as a financial analyst at Grameen Bank.
>
> We had, collectively, nine applicants who had worked at BCG, Bain, or McKinsey.
>
> Four applicants overall had strategy experience in development finance and microfinance.

We selected none of them.

Why is that?

Our model is ground-up development. We look for people who are generally smart, take charge without being bossy, and are very ethical. We do not want to train anyone with these skills who will go on to wreck a company, country, or industry.

You will see the training and investment we are making in these interns. It is material, but our model is to release them back into the market at the end of the internships.

Why would we do that?

Our alumni model is the source of our strength. Releasing the interns feeds and strengthens our alumni network.

Many will remember what we did for them.

They will remember the training and values we exposed them to.

They will draw us in as they move into more senior roles.

So, it is a long-term play. Bring in talented professionals when they are very young and ground them in our way of thinking so no matter where they go—McKinsey, Morgan Stanley, BCG, GE—they remain our alum first and foremost.

This willingness to release people before they peak (because we have the next group ready to take over) is another lesson from Sir Alex Ferguson. It's best not to release an asset at its peak.

Yet another lesson from Sir Alex Ferguson.

BAD LOSERS

We also look for "very bad losers."

You have to have raw talent, work very hard, and have an internal drive not to settle for second best.

One tactic we use is to constantly move the goalposts. Let's assume we set a goal for this engagement, which we have by the way. Once we get to a point where we think we can achieve that goal, we set the bar a little higher.

WEEK 0: PLANNING

We tell the team about the new goal, but not the client.

The client must see the new goal as over-delivery, and he will not view it that way if he knows in advance, we are trying to do this.

Expanding the goal does not have to mean doing more. Expanding the goal could mean developing a deeper insight on a topic or even narrowing the scope of work.

More means better. More does not necessarily mean extra work.

We believe in main financial analyses being presented in ten slides or less. We just want the insights. Leave the diary of your day out.

We do not punish the team if they fail to reach the new goal but do meet the older goal.

No, we only get upset if they fail to strive for the new goal.

We believe that every engagement must set a new standard in insights and excellence. We read many reports from Bain, McKinsey, Goldman Sachs and others that are focused on this line of business, and we are convinced that our work will be better.

That is the internal benchmark we have set, and that is what we will strive for.

Will we reach it? We do not know. But we will do our best.

You cannot reach that goal if you are just smart. You need to practice, take chances, fail fast, pick yourself up quickly, and adjust.

But I insist on seeing the team as trying to improve on a constant basis.

That is another lesson from Sir Alex Ferguson. No matter who you are, if you are coasting on your intellect then you have not set a high enough bar.

SPACE FOR THE TEAM'S PLAYMAKER

Albert and the partner will have a meeting today to discuss the value analysis work he will do, which means working out the economics of the microfinance retail structure in the US.

While we must guide him, we need to do so on just the principles of good analysis and teach him the basics. We need to give him the room to be creative and take some risks.

That is key. He will likely not learn to lead with insights if we control everything. It's best that he takes ownership, and we will provide guidance and help him think through issues.

But he must take ownership and show initiative.

The aim of the meeting is to ensure he sees his role the way I see it.

We will know he is being creative when he develops approaches to do things differently from the approach we suggested, but he still achieves the same goal we have set.

The best thing the engagement partner can do is not panic when something goes wrong and step in to fix things. If we do that, he will not grow, not learn how to fix his mistakes and not develop into the playmaker role we expect him to take.

Will he reach his potential at the midpoint of the engagement or with 25% of the time left?

I do not know, but I trust in our system and know it will happen. And when it happens, it will be worth the wait and the risk.

With Albert's role in place, Nimisha will also need to be groomed.

Nimisha must understand that she will be successful if her team is successful. If she tries to do analyses by herself to show her value, then she will have failed.

In that situation, we have three engagement team members doing great work with no leader.

No, Nimisha must be intellectually mature to realize we will measure her on her ability to organize things for the team to succeed.

This is a major transition for most associates going into the manager role. The ability to set up the team for success requires very different skills from doing analyses well.

I will have to guide her on this. She needs to be calm, stabilize the situation, and ensure Peter and Albert have a clear path to succeed.

STRATEGY

PAUSE & REFLECT

> How can you use the lessons from this book to become a better leader and manager?

> How do you define leadership?

> What can you do on Monday morning at 8 a.m. to be a better leader?

> How can you invest in your alumni network to build a competitive advantage?

WEEK 0: PLANNING

39. THE ROLE OF A PARTNER IS TO MAKE THE CLIENT SUCCESSFUL.

Changing a firm based on the feedback of consultants who should be managed out is a common mistake.

NEVER RELINQUISH CONTROL

Managers should not relinquish control. This applies to partners like me who are overseeing the entire engagement, the engagement manager controlling the team, or an associate managing an analyst.

Very often we receive complaints from disgruntled new consultants and interns that they did not have the "freedom" to do their work or their "opinions" were ignored.

The interns want to choose their own training modules, they want to pick their own streams of work, they want to have complete control over the analyses.

The day that happens is the day the engagement is dead.

When you are managing a multimillion-dollar engagement with multibillion-dollar repercussions, you cannot lose control.

Just because an intern thinks they know better does not mean they do. Some partners and managers take the empathy role a bit too far when they want to sit down and discuss every single concern with the intern. This is touchy-feely stuff that takes up so much time and emotion.

There is a time and place for that, but if the intern's feelings are causing delays that are impacting the engagement, then the intern must go.

WEEK 0: PLANNING

If you look at any one of the many detailed training videos we have on mentoring, you will see that while we will do everything possible to groom a consultant, that act of being groomed is not a right. It is a privilege, and the intern must demonstrate they deserve the investment.

If an intern is disrupting an engagement or is damaging the control the partner has, they will have to be removed.

An intern must control what they are given to control, but the partner is going to set the overall direction and that should not change.

PAUSE & REFLECT

> How do you know the training to select if, early in your career, you don't yet understand the skills of the top performers in your field?
> When and how should partners take feedback from the consultants?
> How do you ensure the changes you are requesting are for the good of the firm?
> How will you convince your firm to include a pilot Week 0 planning phase?
> What is the agenda and tools you will use for Week 0?
> What are the deliverables for Week 0?

WEEK 0: PLANNING

WEEK 1

5 *days*

FIRST FOCUS INTERVIEW, TOP-DOWN FINANCIAL ANALYSES, BONDING WITH THE CLIENT, SHADOW ENGAGEMENT, AND LESSONS FOR A BOUTIQUE FIRM.

FIRST INTERNAL UPDATE MEETING

week 1: INTERVIEWS AND ANALYSES

---

1. THE FIRST FEW DAYS ARE CRITICAL TO SET THE DIRECTION OF THE ENGAGEMENT AND ANALYSES.

The eventual success of an engagement can be traced to those first few days.

PLANNING WITH A DEADLINE

Today is the first day of the engagement. Everything you have read thus far is the planning and buildup. You can see how useful planning is by the effort we have taken to explain how we arrived at the first day of the engagement.

This is the email I sent to the team a few hours before the engagement began:

> "Colleagues,
>
> This is it. In a few short hours, we will begin one of the best ten weeks of our lives.
>
> This is not about you.
>
> This is not about me.

STRATEGY

> We have been training for this our entire lives.
>
> It is bigger than us. This is about our families. This is about our parents and our grandparents, who sacrificed so much before us to give us the great opportunities they did not have.
>
> We could not help them, but we can help those like them.
>
> We cannot predict what will happen in the next ten weeks, but I can promise you people will remember we were here and the impact we made. Let's leave a legacy.
>
> Let's do this for those people that we care about.

We added a Week 0 to the engagement. The interns had three days of onboarding and, rather than using generic examples, we used real LAB public data and issues to train them.

Therefore, we have actually done most of the Day 1 work in the training.

That is the value of having a proper onboarding. Partners must respectfully and politely push back with clients who may not see the value of paying for this.

Engagement managers must try to at least get a few days from partners versus arriving at a client cold.

It is unfortunate in our profession that many consultants take enormous pride in being the person who works until Sunday night on one engagement and arrives Monday morning to start a new assignment.

Good planning costs money, but the returns make the investment worth it.

One way I had of proving the value of Week 0 was to invite Guillermo to the final day, and it went well. We had a really nice open conversation and brainstorming session, and he could see the value of the process.

WEEK 1: INTERVIEWS AND ANALYSES

If there is one thing you should do after reading this much of the book, it's to convince your firm and client to carve a billed onboarding week of at least two full days. An entire week is a luxury, and you are unlikely to get this.

Yet two days is possible. And if you can show the benefits this time, you may get three days or four days the next time.

Just start with something.

Day 1 is crucial on any engagement, but it becomes especially critical when the team has no background about the engagement and even more so when they have no background in strategy consulting.

The team spent the weekend before Day 1 working on their hypotheses, data analysis plans, and storyboards .

I have reviewed them, sent my feedback, and used their data analysis plans to consider any adjustments to the focus interviews.

Finally, I saw their charters on Sunday night. That is their contract with me.

Issue maps (see **Exhibit 14**) are a critical way to manage the streams. Each stream must have this up by 9 a.m. on Monday morning. It is a very powerful, visual technique to communicate and help me manage the engagement.

Imagine walking into the engagement room and at one glance being able to see exactly what is happening by viewing these posters up on the engagement room walls behind each team member.

The team updates their issue maps in real time since the printouts can be replaced on the poster. They are not glued but sit on the poster since it has a sticky finish.

This simple tool is used to effectively manage teams, plot the storylines, and more.

STRATEGY

EXHIBIT 14: Issue map for a single work stream

Issue maps can be designed in any way but must be consistent for the same task, like stream updates

VALUE ANALYSES STREAM

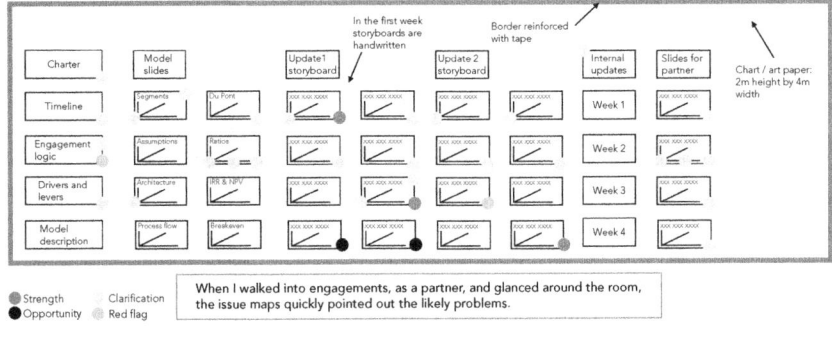

● Strength   Clarification
● Opportunity   Red flag

When I walked into engagements, as a partner, and glanced around the room, the issue maps quickly pointed out the likely problems.

Some interns like issue maps; others don't:

Albert: This is definitely going to slow me down and not help me as much. Can I skip the issue maps?

Partner: No, it's necessary.

A: But I don't think it adds to my efficiency. I have to make the map and update it as my slides change, which takes time.

P: You're right. But it helps the overall team efficiency. How much time do you think will be wasted if each person, including myself, will need to email the other person each time we need to see the latest charter, timeline, engagement logic, and updated slides?

> **A:** Can we not just have a meeting for that?
>
> **P:** Why not skip the meeting for that? And what happens if something in the slides cannot wait until the update meeting in a week?
>
> **A:** But can't I just tell you what matters?
>
> **P:** How do you know what matters to me and everyone else on the team on each day as we learn new things from the engagement? If you don't have time to prepare the issue maps, how will you have time to think about each team member's daily needs and send them emails?
>
> **A:** Okay. I see your point.

Given the progress we are making, we have asked Guillermo to see if we can commence the focus interviews on Monday afternoon.

This could put us in a great position to validate some of our initial hypotheses, so we are very much looking forward to that.

Albert and the partner will make up one team, and Nimisha and Peter will be the second team.

We will have a daily team meeting at around 8 a.m. each morning. It could be around 9 a.m., depending on when the entire team arrives.

Each meeting is mandatory.

The meeting is about managing team morale. It will be just ten to fifteen minutes maximum and will focus on two things:

Nimisha must come up with an icebreaker exercise every single morning. These light conversations are fun, help the team learn about each other, dispel stress, and get people to laugh! With all the stress, we need time to laugh.

We spend a few minutes going around the room making sure everyone is comfortable with the pace and progress, and have the support they need, using **Exhibit 15**.

EXHIBIT 15: Team weekly / daily update report

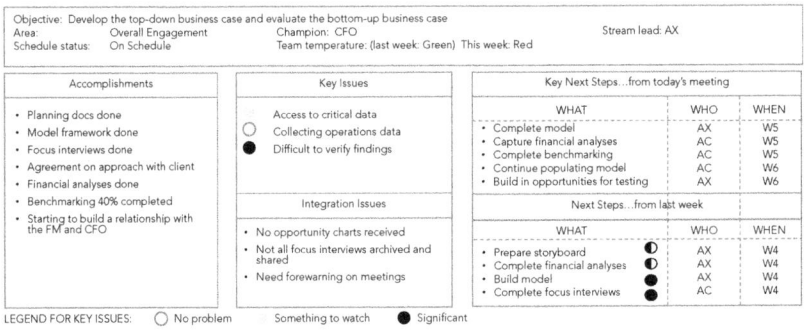

This short exercise is a critical way to show the members of the team that their well-being matters. I generally do not cancel this meeting, except when we physically cannot be together.

In that case, if the team is together, they should proceed without me. That said, in most cases this meeting will take priority over anything else I may have to say.

PAUSE & REFLECT

> How can you keep your engagement team updated while minimizing meetings, emails, and workshops?

> How can you institutionalize the tools, techniques, and best practices from the first pilot Week 0?

STRATEGY

WEEK 1: INTERVIEWS AND ANALYSES

2. BASICS, BASICS, BASICS.

If you know the fundamentals of problem solving, you can learn to be creative later.

BASICS

Even if the McKinsey Worldwide Managing Partner were to retire and start his own firm, it would still be a boutique firm. No matter where you work, when you leave and start consulting through your own firm, it is a boutique firm.

If you work at a boutique firm or a tier-2 firm, or you work for a smaller client at a top firm, the problem you face is that you must eventually serve the most demanding clients, or you will fade into obscurity.

Unless you serve the most demanding clients, you run the risk of becoming conditioned to being great at serving easy clients. And when you eventually serve a demanding client on a complex issue, you will unravel fairly fast.

This creates a bit of a chicken-and-egg problem: You need a top client to learn how to handle them, but you usually need to know how to handle a top client before you can work for them.

The solution: intense and realistic practice. Notice how much effort and time we dedicated to onboarding. That is how you prepare. Too many firms see training as a "nice-to-have" feature.

In the area of consulting, there are some key observations:

1. Many consultants try to perform heroics on an engagement by learning complex analyses. That is a bad idea.

2. You will notice how we drill and train interns in performing the basics very well.

3. We will then train them to handle the engagement under pressure.

4. Finally, we give them the freedom to be creative, then wait for the heroics.

5. You cannot do great things on an engagement unless you know the basics extremely well.

Here's an example:

> **Albert:** I'm going to use AI principles to build the model.
>
> **Partner:** Why not just build a simple Excel model that answers the question?
>
> **A:** AI is the future. The model will be more sophisticated.
>
> **P:** Okay, what are AI principles?
>
> **A:** The model will look for patterns and predict defaults.
>
> **P:** So, the model will simulate the loan book, predict loan patterns, and optimize revenue?
>
> **A:** Yes. The client will love it.
>
> **P:** Check two things. 1) Can a single model simulate, optimize, and predict at the same time? I don't think that is possible. 2) Think about the objective of this model. You are making it far too complicated. Don't turn the model into the deliverable.
>
> **A:** I think it will work.

> **P:** To find patterns, the model must have access to a vast database that is similar to the US market. How will we get that? LAB does not have it and the retail banks will not share this with LAB.
>
> **A:** I did not think of that.
>
> **P:** So, take time to plan your model. Only build what you need to build.

If I shook you up at 3 a.m., I would want you to be able to break down and structure a problem from first principles. I don't need a rundown of vague AI sound bites.

It is a bad sign when the team is doing slides at 9 a.m. on a Saturday morning. That is not expected of them since a weekend is a time of rest.

However, they must acknowledge emails without delaying the study by days. There is no excuse not to be checking emails on the weekend.

A cursory "Thanks" or "On it" is fine. But no responses over the entire weekend is not a good sign.

Even hiking trails have cell phone signals.

Whom the gods wish to destroy they first call promising.

In other words, let's not call this engagement team promising. Let's act as if failure is just around the corner and we have every possible contingency plan in case something goes awry.

STRATEGY

PAUSE & REFLECT

> How are you mastering the basic critical problem-solving skills?

> When do you know you have reached mastery?

> What skills do you start building in each level of your career, such as business analyst, associate, engagement manager, associate partner, partner, senior partner, management committee member, etc.?

WEEK 1: INTERVIEWS AND ANALYSES

3. FOCUS INTERVIEWS GUIDE THE TEAM AND HELP BUILD CREDIBILITY.

This is an important step of an engagement.

PLANNING

The first focus interview is scheduled for 9 a.m.! It's an early start working our way through traffic on the highway.

That means the team must be at the office by 6:30 a.m. to finalize some of the documents, and we will hit the road at 7:45 a.m. to get to our first location by 9 a.m.

The partner will spend all of this morning, before the team arrives, doing the following:

1. Checking the overall decision tree built off the objective function or key question.

2. Ensuring we prioritize the correct branches.

3. Ensuring the team built the correct hypotheses and sub-hypotheses from those branches.

4. Checking the analysis plans to test the hypotheses.

5. Ensuring the focus interviews are both broad enough to capture issues we may have missed and specific enough to capture key feedback to validate some of our initial hypotheses.

That means printing the document and just staring at it. That is how you achieve some level of serendipity.

Normally a senior partner does not do this. The engagement manager should be able to handle this and, if needed, the associate principal would lend a hand. Yet we only have interns with no experience. So, I have to serve in those roles.

Our first focus interview is relatively easy.

We are meeting one of the world's foremost Ivy League experts on development finance in emerging economies. It seems as though such a person would not be living in a city with one of the highest median household incomes, but rather in a village somewhere in Africa or Southeast Asia in order to study his subject area in depth.

Writing about development finance must pay very well.

WHY IS THIS OUR FIRST INTERVIEW?

Two reasons:

> First, we need to test our questions and ensure they do not sound ill-considered or ignore an obvious issue. So, we are picking someone we know who will help us versus criticize us.
>
> Second, the technology we are using makes this essential. We are documenting the focus interviews as they happen for our members and converting them into this book. So, one person will do the interviews while the second person will watch as the software transcribes the interviews (yes, we're not taking notes).

This should be relatively easy to do, but we still need to test it in a real situation. You do not want technology problems in front of a future hostile interviewee, and I want to be sure the interns know how to act if there is a bug in the system.

Should they start furiously typing away on the iPad screen, calling customer support, or sighing loudly, things can get distracting fairly quickly.

I expect I will be dispensing with plenty of behavioral feedback during these next few days.

We will measure and track the team's performance each day and week. Daily spikes or dips are not significant. Look for the weekly trend and overall score.

The partner missed the team event on Friday evening, after falling asleep in his hotel room between 10 pm and 7am.

So, for the engagement partner, fatigue is going to be an issue:

1. This engagement is tough enough since it means managing a complex strategy.

2. Training fresh young interns doubles that problem.

3. Having no experienced consultants on the team makes my role even harder.

4. Managing the process to create daily updates for this book triples the fatigue, stress, and work.

The process of creating all the material for the book makes the engagement much more demanding.

CLIENT MANAGEMENT

Communicating with clients takes time to master.

We have to manage Guillermo, Andreas, and the CEO, not to mention the LAB executives and internal strategy unit. I follow a very nuanced and finely tuned strategy of not expecting the client to say no to us.

Basically, we condition clients and others to treat us in a certain way. We can choose what that way will be. Using my strategy, I initially prefer not to do or say anything such that the client could have an opportunity to push back and say no. If they say no once, they will say no again and again because they think we will accept this.

Therefore, I first build a relationship and slowly introduce complex or controversial ideas. Note, this is not about shying away from debate. This is about knowing when and how to have the debate to get the answer you seek.

This is called the no-negative-precedents strategy (see **Exhibit 16**) because you are not allowing the client to set a negative precedent.

I start the relationship at Step 1 and then gradually work my way to Step 4. This is pretty much how I build relationships with all tough clients.

EXHIBIT 16: No-negative-precedents communication strategy

Follow a strategy called "no-negative-precedents" when dealing with clients

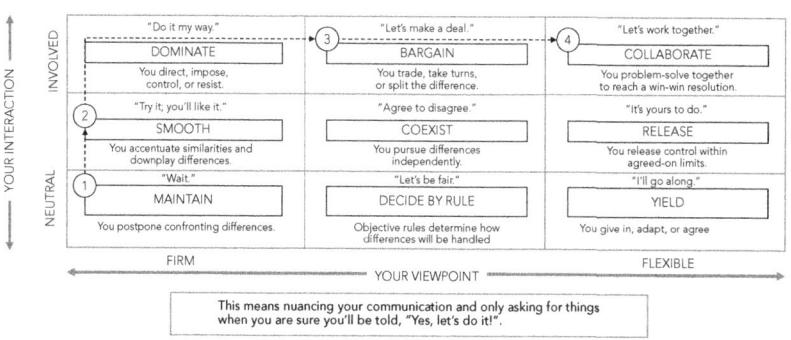

REMEMBER OUR STRATEGY FOR THE ENGAGEMENT?

Our strategy means ramping up the engagement so fast and with so many insights that we overwhelm the negative people trying to stop the analyses.

We explained this concept in great detail earlier under the Ranatunga Doctrine versus the Powell Doctrine.

Of course, we assume we have the stamina to ramp up fast and sustain that blistering pace. I hope the interns are resting.

Remember, it is not about the analytics alone.

Anyone can do the analyses. It is about the way we craft the analyses that matters, and how we draw the insights.

In other words, any firm could complete the analyses we put together, but almost no firm could arrive at this set of analyses unless they saw our approach.

This is a crucial distinction between the best firms and other firms. Our approach is very different.

Everyone is assembled at the client site in our very nice offices, which are on the same level as the client executive team, sampling coffee from the amazing espresso machine inside the office, courtesy of the client. How often do clients give you the gift of freshly made espresso?

So, everything is done.

We started the morning going through the questionnaire and finalizing the document. We finished that fairly quickly and then spent the next twenty-five minutes trying to figure out how to connect to the snazzy cloud enabled printer in our office.

Now that is done. Wi-Fi is also up.

PAUSE & REFLECT

> How can you improve your strategy for building relationships with clients?

> How do you build relationships that last years, even when engagements that are not considered successful?

> How do you mend a damaged relationship?

STRATEGY

4. CREDIT GUARANTEES ARE QUICKLY IDENTIFIED AS A POTENTIALLY LARGER PROBLEM.

This product is out of the scope of work.

FIRST INTERVIEW

The first interview is done, and we had about one hour and twenty minutes. It was a success for several reasons:

1. The focus interview dragnet worked to scoop up a major issue.
2. It seems we are not the only ones who have reservations about the planned model of entering the US.
3. This type of engagement has not yet been done in the US, so our findings will be very interesting.

SECOND INTERVIEW

At 1 p.m., we met the SVP and EVP of the Retail Credit Division of a major retail bank. This bank is a LAB client. The retail bank offers entrepreneurs loans that LAB "guarantees." If the loan defaults, LAB covers most of the default, and if the loan is repaid in full, LAB and the bank make money.

Sounds a bit like a "heads I win, tails you lose" proposition.

This is a key interview because we cannot fathom how this financial product works, let alone makes any money. It sounds like free money for the entrepreneur and retail bank since LAB is the only one paying.

We're thankful that this bank had a nice lobby with powerful air-conditioning.

We learned the following from this great interview:

1. LAB is bearing most of the risk.

2. Bank (singular so far) is not even trying to mitigate losses.

3. Expects LAB to spend even more money to limit losses.

4. Something is not right here.

Now we remain convinced there is no chance the credit guarantee program can be creating value.

The principle of moral hazard applies: Without any real loss, the retail banks have no incentive to manage the risk.

I am surprised to see the retail banks talking to the largest DFIs because these are distribution competitors. They seem to be sharing best practices.

Though we need to be painfully impartial, it does appear the retail banks are almost overindulging in LAB's generosity.

The flip side of this is that LAB is not properly managing their products and guarantees.

The retail banks will do what is beneficial for them, and LAB should structure the products better to manage their risks.

Now back to the office to check the credit guarantee numbers. The partner will not be attending the other two interviews scheduled for today.

Is the retail bank greedy?

No, it appears that the credit guarantee product is simply poorly developed by LAB. It is not the retail bank's fault that such a product exists.

The retail bank's lack of effective risk loan management procedures should again be covered by proper service-level agreements (SLAs) with LAB. That they do not exist is again LAB's fault. The client should be demanding that the proper controls and procedures are in place.

PAUSE & REFLECT

> Do the initial hypotheses change based on the answers from these two focus interviews?

> How would the hypotheses evolve?

> How does the engagement approach ensure we identified unforeseen issues like the credit guarantees?

> What lessons about our approach to identifying and verifying the critical issues could you apply in your own engagement?

WEEK 1: INTERVIEWS AND ANALYSES

STRATEGY

5. WHEN COMMUNICATING WITH A PARTNER, THINK ABOUT HOW TO HELP HIM OR HER, NOT YOURSELF.

Your thinking must be data-driven; just make sure you know how to interpret the data.

PASSING THE BUCK

Never send the partner any work to review that does not meet your standards.

If you send me something, and you do not feel it meets your standards, that is almost a crime and. displays poor judgment.

Why? Because it reveals inefficient and terrible teamwork. If you know something is badly done, why send it to the partner or anyone for that matter? It demonstrates a lack of ownership and accountability.

It is a bad habit.

Do not tell the partner "I read all the material, and this is the best practice, so I think this is what we should do."

Nimisha has picked up this phrase, which many consultants love uttering, but it is flat out wrong and annoying.

It is a cop-out. When you say this, you are basically saying:

"I did not think, so I looked at everything out there, I do not know if it is right, but the supposed leader in the field does this and, therefore, I am following it."

My immediate response to this phrase is, "But why is it best practice, why does it work, and how do you know the conditions for it to work apply to this engagement?"

If you say, "All the experts say it is right, I read it on many forums and everyone agrees," you are basically digging a much deeper hole for yourself.

You are hired to explain things. Yes, the so-called leader in the industry does it, but why do they do it? Moreover, do not repeat the marketing spin generated by PR departments. Explain to me, using simple logic, why this best practice will work.

If you use the quote above, you will struggle as a management consultant.

We are paid to think, not do literature surveys and recite marketing phrases.

Be a thinker, not a processor.

The biggest problem with many consultants is they think they are safe if they copy practices used by so-called industry leaders. That approach may save you in an argument with some Joe Six-Pack in a nearby pub, but it is going to get you into a lot of trouble with a partner, and even a client.

COMMUNICATE PRODUCTIVELY

When most people communicate, they are not trying to be productive. They are actually trying to save themselves from being fired, and they do not even know they are doing this.

For example, we asked one of the associates why he changed the print schedule, he said it was because the client needed the files by 2 p.m.

STRATEGY

Rather than focusing on whether the client received the files, he dug through his email and found my request, which he interpreted incorrectly.

Now the problem with this approach is that he was so obsessed with saving his career that he wasted all that time digging through emails when he should have been following up with the client to see if they had received the documents.

Never try to save yourself; save the client. That is what matters.

Do not confuse process superiority with logic, and the latter with creativity.

You will probably not be a great strategy consultant if you can just follow a process. Which is what most people do.

You will probably not be a great strategy consultant if you are just logical. Anyone can be logical.

You must show creativity that meets the rules of logic.

This is something we am trying to teach the interns.

Creativity is key.

"We can save the client 5% of the costs and have, therefore, done well."

Phrases like this hurt our credibility as professionals. When people are under pressure, they do just enough to show they've met the client's expectations. We were not brought in to hit some average target of 5%!

Internal teams can do that.

We get worried when teams want to settle for mediocrity just to show some impact—any impact. If your target was 1% cost reduction, then 5% is worth celebrating. But if your target was 4.5%, then 5% is not worth celebrating, and 2% is definitely not worth writing home about.

MORE DETAILS DO NOT MEAN MORE SLIDES OR SMALL FONT

We believe in refining slides until the story is very clear. That usually means fewer slides, less text, but a clearer message.

Somehow many people think more details means more information. It is not the same thing.

I want a deeper explanation of the logic and that does not mean more slides.

STILL, WE STARTED WELL

Five focus interviews done, the top-down financial analyses are being completed, and Peter and Nimisha have paired up to also produce the first cut of some of the focus interviews.

So, we are where we want to be, but I do sense the strategy development is process driven. They sometimes do things because they saw it done in the training but cannot explain how it is linked to the hypotheses. I will need to be to watch for that.

Just because Microsoft created the size 6 font does not mean we should use it.

Why add unnecessary details? We need to focus on the message and not cram in every single detail we can find. The trick is to figure out a way to explain a concept without explaining everything about the concept.

"BUT EVERYONE SAYS…"

Who is everyone? Since when did we rely on everyone's opinion for anything? Surely Fortune 500 companies do not load their strategies onto the internet and get everyone to vote?

Using a phrase like this implies you are lazy and unwilling or unable to explain the logic of an argument. It's best not to speak like this. Especially not to a client.

It is perfectly fine to say you don't know, but it is unacceptable if you didn't take the initiative in figuring out the answer. Estimations, brainstorming, and the like are techniques we have at our disposal to fix things. Use them.

NEVER WORK FOR THE SAKE OF APPEARANCES

If you have finished the work, it is fine to go back to the hotel, provided your team does not need help.

It is not wise to get into the habit of staying in for appearances sake. It does not help. The quality will speak for itself, and we prefer not to focus on volume.

DONE FOR THE DAY

The team will continue with its work, and the partner plans to speed-read through the charter governing the client. You will be very surprised how few people actually read core material like this, so it is wise to be one of the few who actually knows the material backwards and forwards.

The charter is about 150 pages in A4 format, so it is going to have to be some heavy speed-reading.

PAUSE & REFLECT

> How have seemingly innocuous actions mentioned in this chapter negatively impacted your career?

> How would your career improve if your routines focused on solving the problem at hand versus creating a paper trail to defend your actions?

> How can you develop a weekly routine of reflecting on and improving your behavior?

> How can you be creative when following a well-known and proven process?

STRATEGY

WEEK 1: INTERVIEWS AND ANALYSES

6. LAB IS IN A DIRE FINANCIAL SITUATION, DRIVEN BY THE CREDIT GUARANTEES.

Fixing the bank's balance sheet should be the focus versus entering the US market.

TEAM MEETING

The team is meant to be at the client office by 8 a.m. ET. We do not believe in bringing in the teams earlier than needed. Starting at 7a.m. ET is a bit too much since rest is key and the days are tough with excessive interview travelling, which leaves the night to work.

We started on a great high yesterday, exactly as planned.

Albert has completed the high-level LAB financial analyses looking at the trends, key ratios, and more. We will review them in about 10 minutes after the team debriefing, which is happening right now.

So far, the team is doing slightly better than a typical internship group. That is a good thing. The mistakes I mentioned yesterday are common and should in no way be interpreted as reflective of a weak team.

Beginning the team meeting with an interesting icebreaker, for instance, "What is your most embarrassing story?" This definitely gives me a new perspective on the team, especially when one of them has a video of their special event.

The joys of the social media generation.

DRUM ROLL, PLEASE

The top-down financial analyses are in, and this is what we found. Just remember the top-down analysis is crucial for pointing out the potential problems, and this will focus the team. They finish by reviewing the auditor's notes and the auditor's financial statements.

All this is done in twenty-four to seventy-two hours. Taking more time almost always means it is done incorrectly, or the consultant is inexperienced and not sure what to do. It should ideally be done in twenty-four hours because it is not complex analysis. It is simple ratio calculations.

> Of all the financial products that LAB offers to the market for small businesses, DFIs produce 81% of all the jobs created.
>
> DFIs are also the cheapest way to create jobs, with LAB spending just $642 to create one job.
>
> LAB offers six financial products.
>
> Using the credit guarantee product, $33,318 is spent to create one job!
>
> Credit guarantees create just 9% of all jobs or 9,608 jobs.
>
> With equity products (investing in customer businesses), it costs $50,027 to create one job and they create <1% or fifty-six jobs.
>
> Equity funds grew at 369% CAGR over the last three years, which makes sense since it is basically free money.
>
> Credit guarantees are growing by <0.5%. This either means LAB knows these are a flawed product and is more careful about offering them, or there is just no market for them.
>
> DFI disbursements (loans issued) grew 44%.

LAB UNDISBURSED FUNDS

LAB is sitting on 41% of undispersed capital that is now sitting in a bank vault somewhere earning a return that does not even meet inflation. That is, of course, not good.

It means 41% of the capital it wanted to distribute to entrepreneurs has not been distributed.

Two years ago, there was a spike in funds being disbursed. This resulted in undisbursed funds shrinking to 17%. However, disbursements slowed down last year, and the undisbursed funds grew to 41%.

If that is true, last year either LAB received new capital or the returns from the previous disbursements are now sitting as undisbursed funds.

But it is unlikely the returns from the previous business operations could be so high. So, LAB is probably just sitting on a new capitalization from the government.

Our gut feel is that future disbursements will turn into a sour loan book as they are forcibly pumped into the market. Because there will be pressure to release the funds and that pressure will result in poor due diligence of loan application and/or investment opportunities.

If you have a weak loan book and your cash earns less than inflation, the value of LAB shareholder funds will lose real value over the next three years.

ESTIMATED SHAREHOLDER LOSSES

They come in at a staggering $123 million real reduction in shareholder value over the next three years if the loan defaults climb as predicted. That is a big number for any bank. That is a shocking number in the emerging markets.

STRATEGY

KEY FINDINGS – PRODUCING A STORYBOARD

Notice the simple logic and story of the points above.

That is called a storyboard. After reviewing 100 pages of auditor notes and three years of financial statements, that is all we will show Guillermo, along with the accompanying simple exhibit.

As a ratio of the cost to create jobs over the number of jobs, DFIs are the most effective way to create jobs at the moment.

> This is why LAB is so adamant about creating a retail presence in the US. At first glance, it appears to work.

Credit guarantees are showing no growth at all, but they have large capital pools committed to them.

> The alternative to the DFI, using other private banks' retail branch networks to offer funding to entrepreneurs, is not just unpopular, the product is economically flawed.

LAB's under deployed capital base keeps growing and earning negative returns.

> Unhappy shareholders want results, but to get results, LAB needs to push funds and it is doing so with weak controls.

This is resulting in a real negative gain for shareholders.

> And they are about to get unhappier in a few years as defaults likely increase.

We estimate the loss to be $123 million over the next three years.

> When they see a net loss on their funds.

We discussed why we would present the client's story this way:

> **Albert:** Shouldn't I document the process I followed, the interesting findings and volume of the work done.
>
> **Partner:** We don't do that.
>
> **A:** I think it will impress the client.
>
> **P:** No, it will not.
>
> **A:** I don't understand.
>
> **P:** Reviewing 100 pages of auditor notes and a few years of financial statements in just a day or two shows you have the stamina to plough through fairly mundane low-level analytic tasks that can be automated or outsourced to the lowest-cost supplier in an emerging market somewhere.
>
> **A:** But it's useful.
>
> **P:** What the client wants is the answer. They are not worried how you got there, provided you are correct. They don't need to see a chronological sequence of all the steps you took to get there.

No one cares about the time we took, our methodology, etc. All clients want are the insights. The insights must be compelling and meaningful. They must rivet the client's attention.

NEXT STEPS

Albert needs to have the LAB SVP for finance sign off on these numbers. Plus, Albert needs to have the auditors check our interpretation of the notes.

We need to find ways to get the team to understand that no matter how much they are doing now, change takes time and we still have lots to alter.

No matter how many improvements they think they are making, learning a new philosophy for analyses and serving clients is not something that happens in a few days.

PAUSE & REFLECT

> How can you use top-down financial analyses to focus your priorities on an engagement?

> How will the engagement change with this information about credit guarantees?

> How should we use this new information with the client?

STRATEGY

7. IF THE CREDIT GUARANTEES ARE SO LUCRATIVE FOR THE PARTNER PRIVATE BANKS, WHY IS THE PRODUCT NOT GROWING?

This illogical finding makes us question our analyses.

We interviewed the head of credit and loans at TalkFinance, an SMME (small-medium-micro-enterprise) lender. He was extremely candid about his bank's relationship in offering LAB's products, the historical tension between the banks and LAB, and things that should be changed.

One thing that strikes us is that everyone we have interviewed believes LAB cannot make money from funding immigrant entrepreneurs and is doing this as a social imperative.

We will have to determine if this is true.

HISTORICAL TENSION

It was evident from the start of the meeting that a great deal of tension has existed between TalkFinance and LAB. Hector, the head of small-loans banking at TalkFinance, was eager to highlight and explain this before the interview started.

Hector explained that the relationship between LAB and TalkFinance emphasized contractual power rather than partnership. He believes LAB has maintained a superior attitude toward TalkFinance and has not tried to understand their position.

This has been exacerbated through the predominance of accounting-type competencies at LAB with little or no banking experience. A punitive attitude toward TalkFinance claims (requests for LAB to reimburse loan defaults via the credit guarantee product) has not helped.

Hector believes the relationship is moving back to an even keel. This has been due to the departure of some individuals from LAB and an honest discussion with LAB's CEO. It is also evident that Guillermo (our liaison at LAB) has a can-do attitude and enthusiasm for SMME banking that is probably assisting this.

HOW THE BANKS MANAGE THE RISK

Hector believes things can improve further should LAB begin to manage its loan book on a portfolio basis rather than micro-managing individual cases. A focus on portfolio KPIs such as an acceptable loss ratio etc. would be more appropriate and allow TalkFinance to exercise its skills as professional bankers.

Hector makes use of a centralized team of six people to manage LAB finance approval. No credit scoring takes place; intuitive analysis is used to examine all cases.

Wow! That's surprising.

DIFFICULTY OF SERVING IMMIGRANT ENTREPRENEURS

A number of key differentiators make LAB loans difficult to assess for risk:

1. Lack of a personal history to apply behavioral scoring
2. Lack of equity from the owner, resulting in the potential for the financing to be used for individual survival rather than the business
3. Lack of collateral on the individual's part
4. A good assessment of the risk would require assessment of the individual's competence within the industry segment where they are starting their business.

WHERE IS THE DEMAND FOR LAB LOANS?

Almost all LAB loans are brought in through TalkFinance's branch network, at least for Hector's bank. TalkFinance makes use of most of LAB's credit products.

Most of TalkFinance's LAB book is based in the retail sector. Franchise is a particular SMME focus area. The bank believes areas such as construction and tenders are difficult to serve, and, therefore, may be neglected. These could present an opportunity. The bank does not get many agricultural industry, food, and rural applications.

The bank foresees some difficulty moving into many industry segments for two reasons:

1. The criticality and poor state of aftercare, such as mentoring and follow-up to the borrower, which TalkFinance believes LAB must provide.
2. The necessity to provide deep industry understanding during aftercare mentorship, both to assist the SMME and to provide an informed risk assessment to the bank.

STRATEGY

TalkFinance stated specific exposure in the construction industry with the above issues. They have not been able to overcome them.

TalkFinance sees potential for SMME project finance for developments such as housing in Arizona, infrastructure, and more, but this will not result in a sustainable SME business, merely a profitable project.

TalkFinance has concerns that mentorship of loan applicants is misaligned. Some mentors are incentivized based on the loan approval, not the success of the business or repayment. This has two effects:

1. TalkFinance has difficulty assessing the competence of the individual when granting the loan, since the business plan is not his or her own.

2. There is little or no incentive for the mentor to stay and help the lender once the finance has been provided. Therefore, the mentor who prepared the plan is not around to help the borrower execute it once the funding is approved.

Furthermore, Hector had questions regarding new industry segments related to sustainability and growth. Providing project finance may result in the creation of profit for the SMME for the project, but then what? For rural segments in particular, where would customers come from: other existing retailers?

> The banks do not focus on immigrant entrepreneurs.
> They just want a bailout.

As a result, TalkFinance is not overly positive about any new entrant's chances of finding a sustainable opportunity in the US SMME finance market. They believe there is more potential in getting the existing model right.

TalkFinance has heard that the US government is mobilizing funds to cover a bank's excess loss experience (If a bank's loss rises from 3% to

5%, the government would cover the extra 2%). TalkFinance is unsure what to make of this. US politics could play a role.

Where should TalkFinance be more lenient? A potentially bad loan is still a potentially bad loan. The lender also sees zero action on Capitol Hill to see this through and believes this is just a rumor.

What's more, TalkFinance's assessment of a successful loan portfolio's characteristics is not particularly encouraging for a new entrant. The lender believes that its minimum sustainable loan size is $130, 000; the minimum interest rate for a LAB loan is fed plus 3%.

This is far from the survivalist segment LAB was mandated to serve, but in the US market, LAB's goal is profitability, to subsidize the bank's loss-making domestic goals. Still, does LAB have the competencies to successfully compete in the US for a different market.

TalkFinance believes that the normal three-year term of an SMME loan may be too short for a LAB loan. TalkFinance is concerned that, while it can raise interest rates to cover increased risks of LAB loans, costs of managing LAB loans (for example, monitoring, aftercare, and collections) is far in excess of others.

> The banks cannot see the opportunity and just want a subsidy—that is the headline.

LAB loans require more management than typical SMME loans. A normal SMME loan manager will manage between 400 and 500 accounts. An emerging markets manager will manage eighty to one hundred accounts.

Hector emphasizes that there is no shortage of money to fund SMME loans. There is a problem with distribution, administration, and collection.

TalkFinance believes there is potential to improve its cooperation with LAB. They are in the market thanks partly to a policy of social responsibility. The lender believes that things are improving but could be substantially improved through renegotiation of its agreement with LAB. The aim would be to enable TalkFinance to easily claim losses more easily.

This should be done individually with each bank. TalkFinance is not willing to share the experience it has gained with their competitors.

The agreement should emphasize a more equal partnership. An effort should be made to understand what TalkFinance processes and what its systems could deliver. This should be taken into account to mold the requirements of TalkFinance.

It is evident that TalkFinance would relate better to an experienced banker managing them than someone it views as an accountant. The lender believes it needs to work with people who have risk management mindsets.

Hector had come into contact with one of LAB's DFIs in San Antonio, Texas, because the DFI owner banks with TalkFinance. Hector mentioned that the owner was dispirited and frustrated with LAB and would exit the business if he could. This is, by the way, a reminder that these are the privately owned distributors who disburse LAB funds into the market and are LAB's largest distribution channel.

SO, WHAT DO WE MAKE OF THIS?

The banks really do not believe there is an opportunity to lend to immigrant entrepreneurs starting with small businesses in the US.

They will only do so if LAB covers as much as 80% to 90% of the losses.

The banks see this as a social obligation, but the reality is they are not taking on any risk. LAB is doing it.

For its part, LAB was seduced by the sexy risk management systems the retail banks purported to have.

LAB hoped to give banks capital in return for using their risk management systems to find a way to lend to immigrant entrepreneurs.

But the banks are not even using a risk management system. They are just taking losses and getting LAB to refund them. They are taking LAB's money.

YET SOMETHING DOES NOT MAKE SENSE.

The credit guarantees are a poorly crafted product such that LAB takes most of the losses. If we were a bank, we would be pushing out millions of them.

But the credit guarantee product is not growing.

Why is that? That does not make sense.

The banks are clever. They would know a great opportunity when they saw it.

PAUSE & REFLECT

> Why do you think the credit guarantees are not growing?

> Can you develop a way to explain why credit guarantees are not growing, using what we know about LAB and our rules of critical thinking?

> How would you test this hypothesis with the minimum amount of effort and data?

WEEK 1: INTERVIEWS AND ANALYSES

STRATEGY

8. TAKE TIME TO CONSTANTLY ADJUST AND IMPROVE YOUR PLANS.

Things change so often on a strategy engagement that the three-day-old plan is always outdated.

FOCUS FOR NEXT TWO WEEKS

1. Focus interviews with stakeholders in the value chain.
2. Shadow studies of entrepreneurs.
3. Shadow studies of finance companies who borrow from LAB to lend to US immigrant entrepreneurs.
4. First-cut of the case studies using literature analyses (top-down).
5. Top-down analyses of LAB's financials (signing off our interpretation).

We are well on track to finishing this on time. So far, all is going well in the engagement. The client (Guillermo and the CEO) is happy.

We are making marked progress and have already unearthed some very interesting findings.

We just need to keep the momentum going.

PREPARING FOR THE FIRST CLIENT FORMAL UPDATE

While we speak to Guillermo pretty much every day, if you count email and mobile calls, we have our first formal update set for next Friday.

We are sharing key findings as we validate them. At the rate we are going, Guillermo is excited, and I believe the update will go well.

We need to decide what we will present. As a rule, only things that fit within the story will be presented.

We will drop everything else.

Our strategy of a massive start is working well, and we should soon shift to the shadow studies that should generate even more insights.

REVIEWING ALBERT'S SLIDES ON THE TOP-DOWN FINANCIAL ANALYSES

There are some problems:

1. The headline does not tell me exactly what the slide is saying. It is vague. I cannot understand the content clearly.

2. There is no story line between the headlines, which means we cannot see what is happening across the slides.

3. Too many graphs and content. Just one, or at most two graphs, to show the message most effectively. Use lots of space and make things clear. Tiny text is not ideal.

4. Too many errors. He needs to be more careful about using the formatting standards we provide.

5. Too much text is being used. It is not essential to list everything we did. Just state the insights.

FINAL TEAM MEETING FOR THE DAY

Time to regroup and make sure administrative rules are being followed. This is how a firm archives information and ensures nothing is lost. This is a big competitive advantage when done right, like this:

1. Focus interview transcripts must be checked and captured immediately in electronic storage on a cloud server.

2. Major findings must be emailed to the team, preferably the entire transcript should be sent and backed up to our central cloud server.

3. Issue maps should be up by now. Some streams are behind in this critical step.

4. Streams need to talk and share more. There's too much of a silo behavior, which will not work on a corporate strategy engagement.

Small administrative things catch up with you if you do not do them.

Two days into the engagement, they are performing slightly better than many of the best interns.

So, this is a very capable and determined team.

R & R

Consultants typically take pride in working incredibly long hours. In fact, if you work at a poorly managed firm, you will work longer hours.

This is because consultants at weaker firms equate punishing hours with productivity.

Yes, this is a brutal engagement but not because of the time we are putting in.

No one will be working till 11 p.m., except possibly the night before a major update and even that will not happen if I can plan this well and if no major issues occur.

If you are looking for insights, you cannot do it if you are sleepy and severely mentally fatigued all the time.

We do not want anyone working past 9 p.m. unless they really have to. Getting the job done is all that matters.

Partners and managers on engagements who death march their teams through long hours usually do so thanks to:

1. Understaffing.
2. Poor planning.
3. Fear of pleasing the client and wanting to show the team is working hard.
4. Failure to position the engagement as a value-based fee engagement.

PETER AND ALBERT NEED TO WORK MORE CLOSELY

I think Albert believes he will generate his insights alone, and Peter believes his findings from the case studies will only inform the corporate strategy.

Actually, many of Peter's findings will be used by Albert to set assumptions, principles, and even data inputs for his model. Here is how that was expressed:

> **Peter:** I am going back to the hotel early today. Is that fine?
>
> **Partner:** Of course.
>
> **Peter:** I found the ratios for the number of loans to officers yesterday and already checked them this morning. I think they will be helpful.
>
> **P:** Great. Did you send them to Albert?
>
> **Peter:** No, I was going to share that in the update with him at the end of the week.
>
> **P:** So, you want your colleague to spend the whole week trying to collect data you need and already have, but you don't want to share it until a formal meeting?
>
> **Peter:** I will email it to him now before I leave.

So, we would want them to work more closely, but Albert needs to tell Peter what he needs. Not the other way around.

Although we expect most of the modeling data will come from analyzing an actual DFI, we will still need some critical information from the benchmarks and case studies.

DEVELOPING A COMMUNICATION PROGRAM FOR ALBERT

Albert is pretty good. His main weakness is communication, managing his emotions, and time management. The best reward he can get from this engagement, besides completing it correctly, is fixing these three weaknesses.

We will put together a plan to help him and set up a session to guide him. All the material we use can be found in "A Typical McKinsey et al. Engagement" on StrategyTraining.com / Strategy Training apps.

CHANGE TO OUR SCHEDULE

I spoke to Guillermo this morning, and we decided to make a change to our schedule.

It is possible that our findings in the shadow studies may encourage us to explore new questions in our focus interviews with stakeholders in the value chain.

Therefore, starting the shadow studies after the focus interviews may not be best for us.

We need to do some shadow studies around midway through the focus interviews.

Therefore, the shadow studies for entrepreneurs will begin today and the shadow studies for the distribution financial intermediaries (privately owned companies borrowing from LAB to lend to US immigrant entrepreneurs) will begin on Thursday.

We will then use any input from those shadow studies to adjust our remaining focus interviews.

SHADOW STUDIES

Two groups will conduct the shadow studies on US immigrant entrepreneurs:

1. Our readers[35] have offered to help and will begin doing so today in Arizona, New Mexico, Nevada, and Texas.

2. The engagement team will begin tomorrow in California and Florida.

EXHIBIT 17: Shadow studies

We hope to cover all the shaded states in the next few days via shadow studies of immigrant entrepreneurs
SHADOW STUDIES AND FOCUS INTERVIEWS: WEEK 1 AND 2

Dark grey states will be covered by the FIRMSconsulting engagement team and light grey states will be covered by our readers helping the engagement team.

---

[35] "Consulting Lifestyle," 1st Financial Services Strategy Study via Crowdsourcing," https://www.firmsconsulting.com/quarterly/financial-services-strategy-study-crowdsourcing/

WEEK 1: INTERVIEWS AND ANALYSES

PAUSE & REFLECT

> How do you balance long hours with the need to carve out time for critical and creative thinking?

> Why are we doing shadow studies?

> Which hypotheses will the shadow studies help us test, and where in the financial model will it be used?

STRATEGY

9. FINDING MISTAKES IS NOT THE SAME AS SOLVING A PROBLEM.

Don't be a critic.

CRITIC?

This morning Albert was absolutely beside himself because he found a mistake in the spreadsheet analysis done by a LAB financial manager.

The mistake seemed to be the great value Albert had created for the engagement.

But we are sure he is not a New York Times book critic.

Frankly we would not be overly bothered if the spreadsheet had ten errors. Even if the errors dramatically changed LAB's financials, it would not be a major issue for me.

What matters is whether or not the broad financial trend has changed. If LAB was losing money, does it mean they are now profitable? If not, why does the mistake seem so major?

I find this to be a problem with some interns. Students look for a tiny mistake or quirk to show value, but they usually miss the broader message from the data. Many university programs encourage that style of thinking.

The broader message is critical since no engagement ever done anywhere in the world is perfect or was ever designed to be perfect.

WHAT IS TEAMWORK?

A lot of young consultants do not understand teamwork.

Fresh from their MBA study, these consultants have usually taken expensive, lavish trips to places like Spain, Israel, Argentina, and Ukraine to meet government officials and help local clients.

They spend about one week in each location.

They learn about working with other cultures.

But that is not teamwork.

Teamwork is the ability to convince a colleague to change his or her mind to your way of thinking, without alienating the colleague or damaging the team environment. That is also the consulting definition of leadership.

Many consultants do not learn this skill. We would urge everyone to practice this skill.

You need not leave the United States to practice this. You don't need to travel abroad to learn this skill.

GET YOUR REST

One point I drive home to the interns is that they need rest. Long hours, killing themselves without eating properly and not sleeping well is selfish behavior.

It is not the mark of a great consultant and will not be rewarded. It shows poor planning and, on an engagement, where everyone is so dependent on the other, this behavior could lead to fatigue, mistakes and a total meltdown.

It is selfish. Why would you want to do that to your team?

Take the rest you need. You are measured for output, not input.

PUSHING THE TEAMS

We place a lot of pressure on the interns to work better, think smarter, plan better, produce deeper insights, communicate better, prepare better slides and storyboards.

This places a toll on them.

EXHIBIT 18: Engagement progress

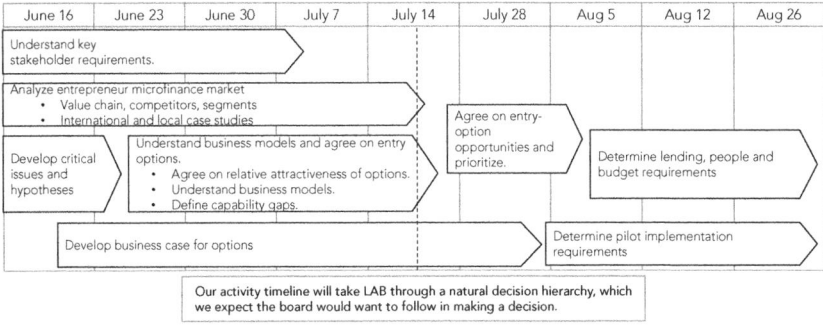

This is turning out to be one of the most complex retail finance engagements we have ever done and one of the most difficult engagements ever.

Pay attention to how we manage the complexity by using the decision trees to break down the issues and build them up.

PAUSE & REFLECT

> What is your definition of teamwork or leadership, and how do you use this to improve the quality of the work completed?

> When you find an error in a piece of work, how do you develop a mindset to extract what is valuable in the work, without unilaterally dismissing it?

> Why do we assume work with an error is not valuable?

> How can we distinguish between irrelevant and relevant errors?

WEEK 1: INTERVIEWS AND ANALYSES

STRATEGY

10. HAVING A BIG EGO IS THE WORST BAGGAGE FOR A CONSULTANT.

Leave your ego at the door.

LESSONS

One of the major decisions we made was to build for the future. We decided to look at what we would need in five or ten years and invest the capital to begin building it, even if it's not perfect.

Consultants and firms in general produce copious amounts of data, slides, Excel files, Word documents, and so on. Most have strange file names, and it is hard to know which is the final version. The majority is not transferred from a laptop to one central archive.

That is mainly because it is such a tedious process to load and describe each file. No one wants to do that. And no one does it. So, over time, a lot of information is lost and information that is archived is rarely used because the tags to describe the files are not really useful.

Nor is the search function useful or the interface to search for files.

So, firms lose all of this information. It is gone forever. We installed a cloud-based storage system where every single document we produce is automatically pulled into one system. And it is an easy system to use and access from a laptop or smartphone.

So, we do not lose information. It is always there and always available in just a few taps on a smartphone. This has given us an enormous advantage because you don't just get the best of the firm today; you get the best of our institutional memory.

Do it even though even it means taking some pain to build something great in the future.

For boutiques and even large consulting firms, there are other direct lessons:

1. Decide where you want to be in three, four, six years and make the investments needed today. The payoff is not immediate, but the return will be clear at the right time. It is best not to lose institutional memory.

2. This is an arms race, but not in analytics. You have to invest in newer, better, and more sophisticated material. Do not bring a knife to a gunfight. It's an arms race to be able to access what you need from any time period as quickly as possible and in the format you need.

3. Great firms take time to build. This is not about taking out cash to buy a Porsche Cayenne in the first year. No, you have to plow back profits to invest for the future. If you want to know how bad infrastructure looks without investment, look at pictures of old Soviet buildings from the 1980s. That is what neglect looks like.

4. Invest in core material. Teaching the basics is important. If you spend $10 million on training but you are not training consultants to think at a fundamental level, the investment is not so useful.

5. Take the long-term view and take the pain in the short-term.

6. Generally, if it is too easy to do, it is not worth doing it at all.

Can you easily use the files you created ten years ago? Ten years ago, you were a smart person. You did good work. You created meticulous PowerPoint slides and word documents. For most consultants, even many firms, that is all gone. It is lost.

Even if those files were backed up, that backup was not maintained, and the files are unreadable.

You may have changed your branding. This means all work before the new branding must be reformatted for the new branding. This is one reason a firm should try to avoid changing its branding.

It's one thing to do great work. You then need a digital system for making sure you can retrieve it. This is something that will only show great returns in a decade, but it is very hard to fix this problem unless the investment is made.

Even large firms struggle with this. Consultants find the process of backing up their files to a central system tedious and most tend not to do it.

WHY AN EGO WILL HURT YOU

Until now, neither the internal strategy unit nor the rival consulting firm have reached out to us.

The act of reaching out to us implies what we are doing has merit.

We report to the CEO, so clearly what we are doing does have merit.

If a partner from a rival firm swallowed his ego and reached out to us, he could very quickly learn about what we are doing and possibly position his firm for more work.

But they will not. You can almost bank on this. None of the major firms will reach out to boutiques run by alums of a rival, nor will they reach out to a firm they consider inferior.

We are obviously using this characteristic behavior to our advantage. How?

We have asked Guillermo's executive assistant not to book any meetings with this firm or the internal strategy unit. If they want an update, I have instructed her to have them call me.

They will not do it. Their egos will stop them because they do not want to be seen as asking for help.

And that delay helps us enormously because it gives us time to conduct the engagement peacefully until we are ready to present.

Remember this. Your ego will kill you as a consultant if you allow it to create a false sense of superiority. Believe you are better but try not to miss an opportunity to learn about a rival engagement. If the tables were turned, we would try to learn as much as possible about this firm.

REMINDING THE TEAM ABOUT CLOSING THE ENGAGEMENT

Weak firms close an engagement and that's it. They may have the senior associate write up the case study and load up a few files, but, by and large, the engagement just ends there. All the key material will likely sit on the laptops of the consultants and will not be loaded onto a global network.

When the consultants leave, the material leaves with the consultants.

Go onto your firm's network and see if you can find the best material from foreign offices. The odds are you will not find much.

Great firms have an intense process post-engagement. All the findings are cleaned, and key data is used to populate one, or perhaps two or three global benchmarking databases. This data is shared across all offices.

The engagement is mined for as much key information as possible.

It does not sit on someone's laptop in the US because the US firm does not trust the consultants in Chile if they loaded the core material onto the internet.

EXECUTIVE FEEDBACK

After four meetings with senior LAB executives, this is the gist of the findings, which was fairly consistent across all the sessions:

1. There was widespread confusion about why LAB is entering the retail market.

2. There was even greater confusion about why the internal strategy unit is preparing for the market entry and we are still assessing the viability of entering the market.

3. The other consulting firm is helping on some aspects of market entry. But we were not informed of this.

4. The executives voiced doubt about the merits of entering the retail market.

5. The client liked the focus of our engagement and the approach, and they felt it was needed.

6. These were very positive meetings, and we were asked to share our findings more broadly since most executives were surprised about our role but found it necessary.

So it was, overall, a good day.

TRAINING THIS WEEKEND

We are going to arrange training for the interns this weekend from 9 a.m. to 8 p.m. on Saturday. This is unusual but I believe necessary. While the team is doing well, the team members are making some basic mistakes and I want to correct this. I want to particularly focus on:

1. Managing clients
2. Communicating with clients
3. Building good storyboards
4. How to operate as a highly effective team

If we did these things better, the engagement could go much smoother. So, a Saturday of work. We strongly believe engagement teams must be well drilled and prepared for the week.

It does not just happen by itself. The engagement partner's job is to make sure the team is drilled on the basics.

At the end of the day, a lot is at stake at the client and we need to deliver. It is foolish to underestimate the other consulting firms here. They are good and we need to be at our best. We need to be prepared for anything, and we need to learn from our mistakes.

I believe it is unacceptable to speak down to or disparage rival firms. Today, we had to caution Albert about his comments about the internal strategy unit.

Our values are what makes us different, not that we are doing the work for the CEO. It is best not to speak ill of rivals because it does two things:

1. It makes you look petty and unprofessional.
2. It blinds you to the strengths the rival will have, and this will have disastrous long-term implications.

Assume a rival is one step ahead of you and plan for that.

STRATEGY

PAUSE & REFLECT

> How do you manage all your previous work as an asset?

> How specifically do you use this asset so that it lowers your costs and increases the value you bring to clients?

> How do you ensure you remember to assess an argument or recommendation or idea on the merits of the thought itself?

> How do you develop the skills to make this assessment?

WEEK 1: INTERVIEWS AND ANALYSES

STRATEGY

11. YOU CAN MAINLY BOND WITH A CLIENT OVER NON PROFESSIONAL TOPICS.

Only in rare cases will clients bond in work-related events.

WRAP-UP

We are done for the day. The team is busy checking its focus interview transcriptions that I will read tonight. I will also complete reading the background articles for our banking client. I am about 75% done.

The team looks a bit tired, so hopefully they will get some well-needed rest. Now it's time to head to my room.

I will have recordings of soccer game playing in the background, all the games I missed, and I'll go through all the work done.

Tomorrow, there will be more focus interviews, more shadow studies, meeting LAB's internal risk group, and preparing for the visit to the two major DFIs. There will be lots to do.

It's an intense engagement, but we are managing it well.

You do not have a great engagement all the time. We need to be prepared and train, so to speak, to manage for the times when things do not go so well. You need to train for those situations when everything goes wrong.

That is why we have scheduled more training this weekend. Just in case things go wrong after our rocking, stellar start.

HOW TO BOND WITH A CLIENT?

This client is obsessed with soccer. I may not be obsessed, but I am probably one of the few people around here who can quote a river of statistics from every World Cup game and the qualifying games.

It's my special skill to remember irrelevant details.

It helps. The client loves it, and we can easily bond. The trick to bonding is to find a common interest and build on it.

In fact, for one of the LAB executive updates, we even had our meeting outside at a bar showing a Spain vs. Chile game. The client insisted and who am I to resist? We did not get the best table, but it was fine.

Mexicans like neither Spain nor Chile, so I was quite reserved the whole time. The trick to bonding with a client is to connect on nonprofessional issues. That is key. It's something most consultants do not pay enough attention to.

Most consultants try to bond on a professional basis with a client and that is a terrible idea.

This is something Kevin Coyne – ex-McKinsey Worldwide Strategy Co-Leader teaches in How to Become a McKinsey Partner, 1st Time Ever Revealed[36].

This is a key insight about building relationships.

---

[36] https://www.strategytraining.com/how-to-become-a-mckinsey-partner-first-time-revealed-full-program

PAUSE & REFLECT

> How can you improve the way you bond with clients?
> What is the objective of doing so?

WEEK 1: INTERVIEWS AND ANALYSES

12. ALWAYS CHECK THE SOURCE MATERIAL.

Sometimes experts are wrong or lazy or possibly both.

MAJOR INSIGHT

LAB was not conceived by an act of government to earn a return that exceeded the inflation rate.

Now that is a finding! So, when the executive posts a loss, the CEO can always say: "But we are just following the legislation."

I am surprised this was even allowed to pass the legislature. It does not compute.

As you can see, being one of probably three people in the world to have read the 200-page law mandating LAB does help.

SCHEDULE

Nimisha and Peter will attend most of the focus interviews today. We have five scheduled for today. I may attend one and will post notes if I do. Note that focus interviews from the engagement are available to FIRMSconsulting Insiders on StrategyTraining.com.

Albert and I will attend a meeting in about 30 minutes with the internal credit risk team at LAB. We want to find out why the credit guarantee products are not flying off the shelf. They should be the most popular products.

Thereafter, Albert will meet the auditors to check our interpretation of their notes. By the way, PricewaterhouseCoopers (PwC) did a great job as the auditors.

If there are no changes, Albert will then meet the head of LAB finance to gain his approval on the top-down financial analyses.

I will review Peter and Nimisha's top-down case studies later today with the intention to shortlist those that we will examine in far greater detail. This involves meeting the companies being studied.

I have a short meeting later today with Guillermo—just 10 minutes—to brief him on the mood of the partners with whom LAB works, mainly the banks offering LAB's products. I need to think about how I will position that message.

Basically, the banks are bleeding LAB, and they know they are doing it. I need to be more tactful in how I deliver that message. That's because these are just anecdotes, and I will hopefully have the verified top-down financial analyses to back me up with hard numbers.

The shadow studies of entrepreneurs in the US continue.

Finally, we are scheduled to go into the field tomorrow to spend an entire day shadowing a DFI in New Mexico. If that is confirmed today, we need to book flight details and finalize all our templates, etc. for the engagement.

It's a big day and a big week. We are well ahead of where we need to be. It is a good day to be a strategy consultant.

CRITICAL FOCUS INTERVIEW

We interviewed with the manager in charge of the LAB credit guarantee approvals and payouts. Probably the smartest person interviewed in the entire engagement.

STRATEGY

She provided the following statistics for the past five years, all in US dollars.

We generally don't like to show raw data, but we wanted you to experience the interview as we did, since it was a pivotal interview.

	2014- #	2014 – $	2015- #	2015- $	2016- #	2016- $	2017- #	2017-$	2018- #	2018-$
Underwriting Exposure- Cumulative	950	129.5M	1214	212M	1518	300M	1636	320m	1604	318.6M
Considered- Cumulative	2717	328M	3426	492M	4324	670M	5010	805M	5617	920M
Lapsed- Cumulative	306	45M	473	81M	596	104M	710	127M	911	164M
Canceled- Cumulative	1003	106M	1084	120M	1202	143M	1370	174M	1614	221M
Expired- Cumulative	199	16M	229	18M	404	45M	640	78M	734	90M
Cumulative Claims Paid	167	11M	245	27M	388	34M	459	58M	610	88M
Claims Lodged- Non-Cumulative							115	17M	244	38.6M
Claims Paid-Non-Cumulative							61	7.2M	127	17.2M
Doubtful Claims Received- Cumulative							522	70.6M	604	81M

The above statistics indicate that:

> Only +- 52% of claims lodged by the banks in March 2017 were, in fact, paid. This has a marked effect on the ability of the participating banks to break even in this area of high-risk lending and is likely to cause ongoing hesitancy to make use of the scheme.
>
> Every rejected claim results in some profit center within the participating bank's SMME areas having to pick up a 100% bad debt instead of a 20% bad debt. As this type of business tends to be fairly centralized, the effect on staff bonuses and increases

can be substantial on the very staff who are being encouraged to lend to SMMEs. Result: less appetite to get involved.

This also potentially explains why LAB products are not flying off the shelves.

As the guarantee scheme under LAB's control ages, the potential claims increase in the future. By way of example, the dollar value of claims paid increased by 70% between 2016 and 2017. Between 2017 and 2018, this percentage went up by a further 52%.

The underwriting exposure of LAB increased exponentially between 2014 and 2016. Thereafter, it tapered off and reflected negative growth during the financial year ended March 31, 2018.

This points to a first-time cost squeeze on LAB as claims continue to rise and guarantee income remains static or declines just a little.

With cumulative doubtful claims of $81 million received by LAB as of May 31 this year and generated by 604 advances, the probability exists that LAB is going to come under ongoing pressure to pay out this amount.

In this circumstance, is LAB sufficiently capitalized for this eventuality?

One of the major reasons for the coming tide of credit guarantee claims against LAB is that only 10% minimum up-front capital by the borrowers was necessary. So, borrowers did not have enough so-called skin in the game. And, in a difficult economic climate where interest rates have risen substantially over the past few years, many LAB-backed start-ups just haven't been able to or have not had sufficiently motivated owners to succeed.

Whatever recommendations are made for the guarantee scheme in the future, it will probably be best to ring-fence the existing position and work the exposure down over time, rather than have these statistics affect the negotiations for any revised scheme to be implemented.

PAUSE & REFLECT

> What are the implications of the interview with the LAB credit guarantee manager?

> Does our engagement approach change?

> Why was LAB not expected to earn a return that exceeds inflation?

> Did the government make an error in conceiving LAB with this inflation goal?

STRATEGY

13. TAKE THE TIME TO ENSURE THAT A CRITICAL INSIGHT IS UNDERSTOOD.

Lack of understanding is a common reason why a client fails to act on a recommendation.

LAB CREDIT RISK TEAM

We had an insightful meeting with the LAB internal credit and risk team.

We believe the credit guarantee products should be flying out of the banks since LAB guarantees 70% to 80% of an entrepreneur's loan if it defaults.

That is a great deal for the banks.

But the product is not growing. Why is that?

LAB's risk team is aware that the retail banks are not properly vetting loan applicants nor following risk procedures effectively. This has been corroborated in the focus interviews with the retail banks where an actual response was:

> "We do not worry too much about checking the applicants when we issue loans since we think most of the work is in the aftercare."

The credit team cannot block a loan from being issued, but they can make it so hard for the retail bank to claim the guarantee that the retail bank thinks twice about offering more poorly vetted loans.

And this is what is happening. The credit team feels the product is poorly structured, and there is little penalty or incentive for the bank to prevent defaults, so the credit team is using its only weapon: blocking credit guarantee refunds to modify the banks' behavior.

But it is not working because the banks are not modifying their behavior. They are simply stopping the issuance of more loans until they get more refunds on defaulted loans approved and they can get LAB to do all the heavy lifting to set up mentors, manage aftercare, and even set up an accounting system for the entrepreneurs.

The credit team may get penalized at Christmas since it is approving far too few refunds but saving a lot of LAB capital.

Somehow, we need to find a way to get the banks to change their model without this confrontational approach used by the credit team.

The credit team is trying to fix the problem after the fact. Rather than withholding refunds, LAB should be involved in the loan issuance process.

LAB wants to do that by entering the retail market in the US.

So, you can see the two reasons why LAB wants to enter the US retail banking market:

1. LAB is not doing as well in its current markets.

2. DFIs are not doing their best at issuing loans, and LAB wants more control over this to speed up the issuance of funding for immigrant entrepreneurs. LAB also wants greater control over the issuance of loans since the alternative distribution mode –working through retail banks—is not working.

The question is: Should LAB enter the US retail space, and can it successfully move from wholesaler to retailer?

MEETING WITH GUILLERMO

Guillermo asked me to sum up our findings regarding the relationship between the retail banks (who offer loans to entrepreneurs on behalf of LAB) and LAB (who will refund 80% of the value of the loan, to the bank, should the loan default) in one phrase/ or word.

The appropriate word could be "greed" or "manipulation." But those would not be terms related to economics.

The term in economics is "moral hazard." If you structure a deal in such a way that party A incurs a minor penalty for extracting maximum benefits from party B, then party A will not change since the penalty to force them to modify their behavior is insufficient.

There is another pop culture phrase for "moral hazard." But we cannot mention it here.

AUDIT APPROVAL OF THE NUMBERS

The financial manager, a chain smoker, is also very pleased that we are highlighting all the key issues.

He feels that we are offering an unvarnished and unbiased view of what is happening at LAB, and he has struggled to get the CFO to present this to the board.

He was surprised we boiled everything down to just five slides.

"Eerie resemblance to the sub-prime crisis.

The banks are lending to immigrant entrepreneurs without proper checks or even follow-ups.

Loans are not even explained in many cases before the entrepreneur accepts.

The banks are doing this because they expect a bailout in the format of the credit guarantee.

Do you see the similarity to the housing crisis of 2008?

When I used this analogy with Guillermo, I think for the first time he understood the issue in a clear way. Use good analogies to explain concepts to clients.

Today's meeting was probably the first time he had seen the numbers regarding LAB's performance in such a simple and clear way.

PAUSE & REFLECT

> What can you do to make a client understand a critical insight and act on that insight?

> As a taxpayer of Mexico, should you be pleased with LAB's performance?

> If LAB was floated on a public exchange, would it be an attractive investment?

> Why would a private equity firm consider investing in LAB?

STRATEGY

14. SHADOW STUDIES RELIABLY TEST THE INITIAL HYPOTHESES.

Participating in just one such study will generate more valuable context than anything you could possibly read.

PLAN

The team will fly out tonight and arrive in the wee hours of the morning tomorrow, around 12:17 a.m. and probably get to the hotel around 1:15 a.m. since the team members have to drive to a US border town.

They will get about six hours of sleep and arrive at about 7:30 a.m. at one of LAB's largest distribution financial intermediaries (DFIs), who lend money to immigrant entrepreneurs.

So, you can see there are two primary retail channels through which LAB serves immigrant entrepreneurs in the US:

1. Massive retail banks and their branch networks in high-density zones south of the US-Mexico border. These banks lend to migrant entrepreneurs who cannot secure funds in the US. They gain funding in Mexico and take the money north to open a business. This is a highly regulated business.

2. Privately-owned, smaller-sized and shorter-term financing businesses within the United States and Mexico who borrow capital from LAB to lend to immigrant entrepreneurs in the US. These are called distribution financial intermediaries, DFIs.

This is the business we are visiting tomorrow. This is an unregulated market and the Wild West of the financial services industry. You may have heard of pay-day loans, but these businesses have escaped detection.

LAB does not have any ownership of these businesses.

LAB offers other products, such as equity investments, but these come through smaller channels like small VC firms or the larger DFIs and retail banks. This is not a big part of their business.

OBJECTIVES

We want to shadow all levels of members—tellers, claims processors, branch managers—throughout the day and see how they spend each fifteen-minute increment of the day.

We also want to see the volumes they process and the technology they use.

On Saturday, the team will go out and spend the day with a claims officer whose job is to track down and follow up on delinquent accounts. Sometimes, they just pay a courtesy call. Training will have to be rescheduled.

WHY ARE WE DOING THIS?

LAB is trying to open up its own retail network in the United States to replace the DFIs because it believes the DFIs are very successful, but lack the vision, capital, and expertise to have a massive impact in the US.

We want to model the economics of the DFIs to determine:

1. What the current finances could look like.

2. What it would look like if LAB entered, and

3. Whether entering the retail market in the US would allow LAB to best meet its dual mandate of profits (in the US only and of a sufficient size to subsidize losses in Mexico) and job creation (job creation only applies to Mexico).

It's going to be a very interesting time in New Mexico. Saddle up pardners! I am just assuming New Mexico has a cowboy culture like Texas. I could be wrong. Hope the interns like fiery dishes.

STRATEGY

PAUSE & REFLECT

> Why have we not outsourced this data collection to a market research firm?

> Why are we visiting the DFIs when we could have easily sent them questionnaires and asked for an audited financial statement?

> What do you expect us to find in the shadow studies?

WEEK 1: INTERVIEWS AND ANALYSES

15. STRATEGY CONSULTANTS SHOULD SPEND MORE TIME THINKING AND LESS TIME ANALYZING.

The common mistake is to spend 90% of the time analyzing data and just 10% thinking about the implications.

TIME TO THINK

As you may have noticed, this is a very complex engagement. Just getting your head around the issue to build a framework for analyses takes time. And analyses themselves take time.

In a strategy engagement, you must carve out sufficient time to think about the analyses, findings, and data.

If you do not do that, you will end up offering the client fairly mediocre advice.

Take time to think. You cannot force the insights and vision.

I take about thirty-five minutes in the morning to review what was done, about an hour during the day and up to two hours at night.

That is almost four hours of reviewing and thinking. It is needed. Do not confuse activity on an engagement with value to the client. They are not the same thing.

That is why I worry when I get emails from readers saying they are working all the time. That is not good for you or the client. A good advisor spends a lot of time just thinking.

PAUSE & REFLECT

> How can you improve your insights by thinking more about the problem, while reducing the time spent analyzing data?

> How soon after you begin an engagement do you begin your analyses, and what would the result be if you dedicated five days up front to planning?

> What changes would you need to make to your rates, billable hours, and staffing model to afford these five additional days?

STRATEGY

16. THE HALO EFFECT IMPACTS JUST ABOUT EVERY ENGAGEMENT.

It is also the reason one carefully checks the methodology and business judgment of the authors.

DESIGN

The secret to carrying out a good case study is to analyze just a few things. Most consultants make their case studies so broad that they cannot take the time to check and verify the facts.

For example, , if you have ten days to produce each case study and you want to focus on five issues in that case study, then you reasonably only have (ten/five) = two days for each issue.

Can you truly understand each issue in just eighteen hours?

Therefore, keep it simple and focus on just one or two things so you have time to digest everything.

Why do consultants go broad?

Mostly laziness. If you go broad, you have a greater chance of collecting a lot of information and, therefore, at least you have something to show the client.

If you focus on just one or two things, then you may not find the information you seek and that will make you look bad to the client and the team.

Being focused takes much more work and discipline.

How did we structure the case study this morning?

Step 1: Determine the key analyses we needed to finish.

Step 2: Identify the data that could not be collected from the information we had.

Step 3: Identify the data that could be collected from case studies.

Step 4: Prioritize that data.

Typically, you will find that we don't actually need much information from the case studies. For example, we don't need to know the volume at which retail channels in other countries break even. We would only need that to provide a benchmark against the break-even numbers we are modeling.

A QUESTION TO ANSWER IN THE FIRST CASE STUDY

I want Peter to answer some very specific questions in this engagement. What I do not want is for him to simply produce what he can find on the internet and Google, which is the way most consultants produce case studies.

This bank went through a turnaround at some point after the Asian financial crisis. What led to the turnaround? Was there an increase in defaults?

Specifically, did it change its operating model, governance, loan structures, and products during the turnaround?

For Peter, it is crucial we get information directly from the bank and speak to people, probably retired now, who were involved in this turnaround. We want numbers and data. Not just war stories.

We cannot emphasize this enough.

WEEK 1: INTERVIEWS AND ANALYSES

We should not rely on reading news clippings. Speak to those who were there at the time, not just today's senior employees.

Many years ago, when I was a partner helping a Chilean mining company restructure, we were struggling to figure out how the client's main competitors kept their costs so low and efficiencies so high.

Plenty of papers had been written about the reasons, but they were really just highly refined hypotheses. We could not allow the client to make any changes until we knew for sure.

So, we kept looking for someone at the competitor who could explain the process. Obviously, no one wanted to speak to us.

Eventually, we found a seventy-two-year-old former executive who the competitors' founders had tasked, over twenty years ago, to set up the mine.

Over three days, this man talked us through the detailed setup he had used to create such an efficient mining structure, which the client still uses today.

You know when someone actually knows what he or she is talking about. It is eminently logical and practical.

From that set of interviews, we were able to model, test, and recommend an entirely new organization structure for the client, which led to a 37% drop in operating costs and a 22% increase in output.

That is why speaking to the key people is essential.

So do not build your entire case study on articles and other cases. You just don't know the competency, objective, or thoroughness of the reporter. These people are under tight deadlines and underpaid. It is incredibly rare for editors to assign sufficient time to truly understand what happened.

Most people are not trained to ask the right questions or even to be critical, and they simply write what they think the public wants to hear.

If you followed that, which is what most consultants do, the client won't know. The client may very well be happy with the consultant's work. But it is unlikely you will find the best answer for the client.

HALO EFFECT

I have noticed that everyone is talking about and copying Google and Netflix's supposedly brilliant human resources policies.

Why?

Here is a sobering question: What if Google and Netflix's HR policies are actually not so good, and the companies are doing well despite their HR policies?

This is not hypothetical. It could well be the case that both companies are just lucky, and the success of a few individuals led to the companies' success. But we prefer to attribute the success to some grand HR design.

No one ever asks the question; How do we know copying their HR practices will not hurt us?

In psychology, this is called the halo effect, where we take one positive attribute of a company, usually its surging profits and growth, and, thanks to a cognitive bias, apply this positive halo to everything a company does. Remember when everyone wanted to copy Enron's HR policy because it was perceived as best in class? That wasn't so long ago.

We have to be careful of this. We see this thinking all the time. People say, "Oh, this is Google's best practice for design, so let's do it." Again,

Google design might be very poor, and the company could be doing well despite its weaker design.

So why copy Google's design?

Coming back to cases, just because a bank is doing well, does not mean all of its initiatives are the reason it is doing well. We have to be very careful to identify the true cause of the effect and not merely copy an initiative just because everyone says it is the reason.

PAUSE & REFLECT

> What can you do tomorrow to avoid the halo effect?

> How can you get your team to avoid the halo effect?

> What must you do to ensure the credibility of your ideas if you studied the case of a firm with a negative halo?

WEEK 1: INTERVIEWS AND ANALYSES

17. BE CLEAR ABOUT DEFINITIONS IN AN ENGAGEMENT.

Assumptions are the main source of misunderstandings.

REMEMBER WHY WE DO THE FIRST CUT?

The first cut of a case study merely involves reading literature, magazines, journals, other case studies, and other relevant material. From this top-down process, we can then select the final list of microfinance institutions where we will apply a much more thorough analysis, including interviews with the CEOs and management.

Most firms only keep their case studies to the level of desktop research. That is a mistake because when you rely on someone else's work, you may suspect they were not so thorough, but you can be sure they were not trying to answer the same question as you.

Remember all those thousands of experts who said Enron was a star?

They said it because no one ever bothered to research it. They simply wrote what they thought people wanted to hear or what they heard or read a multitude of other experts saying.

STATING OUR OPINIONS

We will not, and cannot, take a public position on immigration issues.

Guillermo told me today that he hopes that we really believe in the cause of supporting immigrant entrepreneurs and that we show our support.

That is the opposite of what we should do. We need to be neutral and do what is best for the client—shareholders of LAB.

Our clients are not immigrant entrepreneurs, and we should not allow personal feelings to sway the engagement.

If we allowed that to happen, it would make us very dangerous management consultants.

On this engagement, I have not allowed the client to know where we stand on the issue.

People may think they know where we stand, but they do not.

This is an economic problem pure and simple, and it should be void of our personal beliefs.

My own personal belief, for instance, could be wrong.

WHAT SARA CARBONERO CAN TEACH YOU ABOUT STRATEGY CASE STUDIES

Sara Carbonero is a famous Spanish sports journalist.

Today, I have the distinct pleasure of sitting next to two English gentlemen at a bar. They were engaged in a heated discussion about who was the most attractive female sports journalist in the world.

After about seven minutes of this back-and-forth banter, they asked my opinion since I was the only person nearby.

But they were quite drunk and did not take kindly to my correction, nor is it likely they understood it.

They asked me:

"Who is the most beautiful female sports journalist in the world?"

LESSON 1

I corrected them, and clarified what question they wanted me to answer:

"Who is the most beautiful female sports journalist in the world, whom I know? I probably know different journalists from you."

A small but substantive point.

They did not seem to get this point, made some comment about lawyers being uppity, and continued arguing.

But this is a good lesson in case studies. We typically select the most famous examples in a sector to analyze, versus the most useful.

Like Sara Carbonero, we know her because she is famous.

So, I select from what I know versus all the options. For all I know, there could be someone much more attractive working in Ecuador who has not graced a magazine cover that I've ever seen.

If I do not know her, I cannot select her.

LESSON 2

"Beautiful" is a subjective term.

The same lesson applies to case studies. Do not just pick famous examples in the press like Grameen Bank. Carefully think about why you want to use the case study and ensure the issue represents a central theme in that company's success or failure.

In case studies, it is good to define the term "useful."

So, when you ask people for options to analyze as case studies, remember they are working from a different sample size and have very different criteria for making their choice.

After reading all of Peter and Nimisha's desktop research, the final list of countries we will focus on for the detailed in-person case studies are:

Poland

Indonesia

Bolivia

Dominican Republic

Kenya

Thailand

Bangladesh

Canada

I included a mix of abject failures and alleged successes. Again, in the detailed focus interviews, we move past the interpretation in Harvard cases, news stories, and the like. To do our own primary research to understand whether the venture failed or succeeded, and why, we try to get independent corroboration.

If we cannot corroborate anything, we will not use it in the engagement.

How a microfinance business fails or succeeds is more useful to know than the fact that it did.

So do not simply select the best example. Select examples where the context, sequence of events, and circumstances were similar. If they are not similar, they are at least of a variety that allows you, the strategy consultant, to draw meaningful conclusions and lessons.

This applies to my use of Sir Alex Ferguson examples. It has nothing to do with management consulting, but the context, sequence of events, and circumstances allow me to draw meaningful conclusions about management.

Learning from the case study of a company that has not experienced even one-tenth of the challenges your client has faced is not going to help your client overcome its challenges.

MOTIVATING THE TEAM

The team is safely in New Mexico. It is eerily quiet at the client office. I will be working on the update for next Friday and thinking through one of the case studies.

I want to show Peter the level of analysis I seek and the level of confirmation I require. In this way, he will know what "good" looks like.

At this point, we have finished twenty-one focus interviews, thirty-three shadow studies of entrepreneurs and, by this Sunday, all two shadow studies of the major DFIs. The top-down financial analyses are done.

We are actually in a very good position without having had to resort to stressful hours.

That said, we will have to shift our training back from Saturday to a much shorter Sunday, kind of an extended lunch session since the team will be tired after working on Saturday.

Match the message to the moment. There are different ways to get the improvement you want from a team.

Sometimes it means regaling them with anecdotes from your numerous previous engagements. They are covered extensively in our library of +480 podcasts[37] and our membership library of more than 6,200 episodes on StrategyTraining.com and Strategy Training apps.

---

[37] https://www.firmsconsulting.com/podcasts/

Other times, it means taking a tougher stance with deeper training. Or it just means letting them figure it out for themselves.

The trick is to know when you are pushing the team too much and to alter your style accordingly. If you use the same style and tactics to motivate all people, the chances are it is not working.

Working on a weekend is a big sacrifice for anyone. If I behave as though this is expected of them and I do not appreciate their time, there will be a loss of respect and a feeling of resentment.

I need to show them that I acknowledge their sacrifice and I am grateful for it.

In this way, they will be willing to do the same later because they know their efforts are appreciated.

So, I will take them out for lunch on Sunday, and we will have a general discussion about general interests.

THE MYTH OF COMPLEX ANALYSES

Many aspiring strategy consultants, be those in MBA programs or corporate or internal strategy units at companies, take immense pride in producing complex analyses in their attempt to solve a strategy problem.

That is a dangerous practice and a myth about how we operate.

The engagement we are doing at the moment is very complex. It is easily up there as one of the toughest engagements I have led in my career.

But the analyses are not complex. The complexity lies in framing the problem, asking the right questions, and developing the correct hypotheses.

I need to determine the set of analyses to perform and the sequence and order in which they need to be done.

In fact, the complexity is about making the questions logical and choosing the sequence of the analyses. That is the hard part, not the analyses themselves.

What an outsider will see at the end of the engagement is a complex set of analyses, but if you break the overall analyses into their component pieces, they are fairly easy to do.

It is like building a car that consists of 24,000 individual components. If you tried to hold the entire blueprint in your head, it is impossible.

But if you had the sequence schematics that showed you how each piece came together and in which order, it is easy to build the car.

Thus, in doing your analyses, do not aim for complex studies for the sake of doing impressively complex studies. You need to design an engagement that is just good enough to answer the questions being answered. Focus on the questions. The right answer to the wrong question is still wrong.

WEEK 1: INTERVIEWS AND ANALYSES

PAUSE & REFLECT

> How do you know when you've done just the right amount of analysis to support your recommendation?

> What are your criteria for selecting an issue, event, attribute, or organization to study as a case?

> Why do we assume a framework can solve a complex strategy problem, for instance, to tell us what GE should do?

> Why do so many consultants search for frameworks but rarely the tools to pull together and understand the analyses?

STRATEGY

WEEK 1: INTERVIEWS AND ANALYSES

18. THE VALUE OF ONE INSIGHT IS GREATER THAN THE VOLUME OF INSIGHTS.

One long and difficult trip can yield one critical finding.

DAY 6: NEW MEXICO

Day 6 begins in New Mexico for the second leg of the DFI visit by the engagement team.

Nimisha has done a great job of growing into her role to the point that I can manage them remotely during field visits.

It's 7 a.m. and I survived last night's many rounds of sake with a sober mind and hung-over liver. Though I may not be able to visit a Japanese restaurant again in the near future. All that sake created a blur of pastel colors.

From Nimisha's notes taken during the visit to the distribution financial intermediaries in New Mexico, we deduce:

Very basic offices with little technology and just three employees: a manager and two employees to process claims, speak to immigrant entrepreneurs, answer the phone, and the like.

The office is paper and process intensive. Most steps are not digitized, and processing one loan application takes substantial time.

The DFI does not centralize its risk-scoring system, so it is not learning from past experience. It is heavily relying on the local employees to know and assess the applicant.

STRATEGY

The manager spends 35% of the time on verifying the fieldwork forms submitted by agents in the field, see **Exhibit 19**, and 35% of the time going into the field to support agents.

The DFI owner's daughter visited the branch today in her Mercedes GT Coupe.

EXHIBIT 19: Shadow study: the regional manager

The regional manager's role would be redundant with basic reporting software, which would standardize processes
REGIONAL / AREA MANAGER ACTIVITY TIME

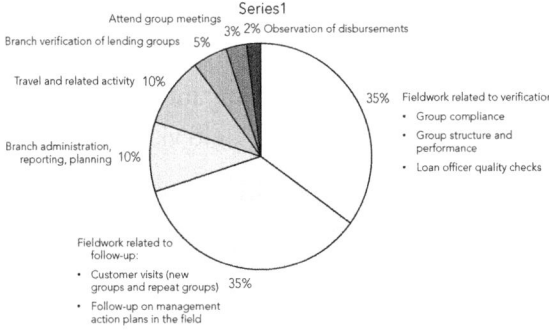

There is a good process, but it is slow.

Processes are not standardized. Managers are using their own processes, versus the one process than works.

The focus seems to be on reducing delinquency on payments and defaults. Very little attention to ensuring the right applicants get the loan.

A culture of fraud forces managers to spend approximately 40% of one workday verifying details in the field, see Exhibit 19, and a poor IT system requires them to spend 47% of their time manually reconciling payment details. The manager confirmed this was a typical day for him.

WEEK 1: INTERVIEWS AND ANALYSES

EXHIBIT 20: Shadow study: the branch manager's Tuesday activities

Ninety-four percent of the time spent on Tuesday could have been automated, thereby reducing labor costs
TOTAL WORKING HOURS = 8.5 HOURS

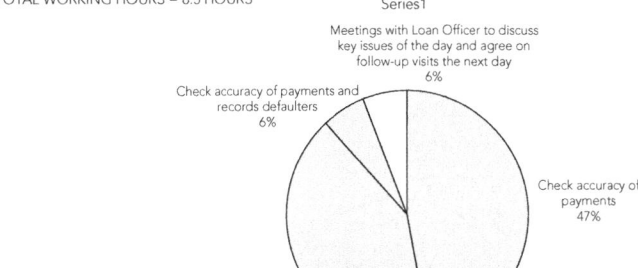

The default rates for the DFI's urban and rural branches are almost exactly the same: This makes sense since immigrants may borrow in one country or state and end up spending it in another country or state. So, the location of the branch is not a proxy for the location of the borrower.

There are question marks about the effort to educate the borrower. In the branches visited, there are no brochures, no advice offered, and in the three application meetings we sat in on, most immigrants did not understand the terms used. One had to sign the documents with an X because she was illiterate.

Among the immigrants, there is extreme fear of deportation, and many provide only mobile numbers, no physical addresses. This makes following up difficult. Even where addresses are provided, they tend to be shared residences.

With soaring loan defaults, very little time is spent on mentoring and follow-up to prevent defaults (see **Exhibit 21**). We saw just 10% of the time allocated to following up on defaulting loans.

EXHIBIT 21: Shadow study, branch manager's Monday activities

Administrative items are taking up close to 50% of the work time across other days as well
TOTAL WORKING HOURS = 8.5 HOURS

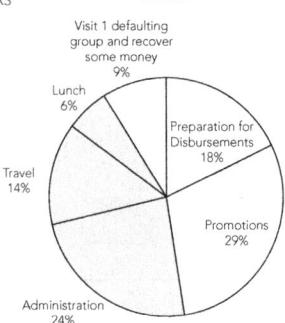

Offices use dial-up internet connections and there are no printers, so loan applications are modified by hand. There is no central repository where the modified loan terms are housed and can be used to adjust LAB's balance sheet liabilities.

Branches only get technology and supplies if they can generate a profit to cover their costs. No profits means no supplies, and the internet is cut off. The manager uses her iPhone as a hot spot and had to buy a wireless router since the aged PCs did not have a wireless receiver. She is not reimbursed for this expense.

Since supplies and bonuses are tied to volume, the branch is under enormous pressure to issue as many loans as possible.

It is not clear, but only the manager appears to be paid above minimum wage. Will need to check that, though everyone seems pretty well dressed and they drive nice cars. That is very hard to reconcile with the numbers our client provided.

DAY 2

Today the team will be shadowing a group of field agents. The agents have several roles:

1. Visit borrowers and offer advice, answer questions, and help in any way they can.
2. Follow up on late payments or defaulting recipients.

One thing we are already seeing is that finding the recipients is tough. In many cases, borrowers are not providing their own addresses but rather addresses of family or friends.

The heat is also oppressive.

We are interested to see what happens when a borrower refuses to comply with instructions. This is a largely unregulated business, so the DFI has much leeway here.

BRILLIANT INSIGHT

Now we know what happens!

This is interesting, so pay attention to what happens next.

When the DFI lends money to the immigrant entrepreneur, it expects to be repaid the principle plus the interest, and a high interest at that.

A $500 loan with interest can cost up to $1,200 in some cases, with very high interest-rate ceilings.

But the DFI makes more money if the borrower defaults. When the borrower defaults, the DFI can enter the borrower's bank account, since the DFI has all the access details and can retrieve the full amount, plus interest and penalties.

The penalties are large because the DFI wants to cover the operating costs of having the agent out in the field chasing down the borrower.

If the borrower repaid the loan after extensive delays, the DFI cannot charge the penalties to recover the agent's operating costs and make less money.

There is actually a perverse incentive to force defaults the longer an agent is dealing with a client because the costs go up the longer the agent works with a client, and at some point, that cost cannot be recovered via the interest rate.

If we ran the analyses, we would see defaults being positively correlated to the time an agent spent with a borrower.

This would be the opposite of what you'd expect. You would expect defaults to go down since you would assume the agent was helping and educating the borrower.

Right here, you see the incredible value of proper fieldwork and not listening to so-called best practices because everyone insists agents should spend more time in the field. But it very much depends on how the agent is used in the field.

If this is true, we should see in our analyses that lower defaults are not correlated to higher profits for the DFI. Higher defaults equal higher profits.

So maybe the solutions are:

1. Better applicant screening so less follow-up is needed
2. Better agents
3. Changing agent incentives
4. All of the above?
5. LAB should run the retail network
6. LAB should partner with an established retail bank in the US and dissolve the DFI model

As you can see, this is complex. Our job is to make the decision easier, so we ask:

1. Is the US market attractive?
2. Is it attractive to LAB?
3. Is the retail structure the best way for LAB to achieve its mandate?
4. If yes, how?
5. If not, what is the alternative?

STRATEGY

PAUSE & REFLECT

> Why do you think this insight about the defaulting loans is key?

> What is the major insight from the shadow studies?

> How will we use these pie charts from the shadow studies?

WEEK 1: INTERVIEWS AND ANALYSES

STRATEGY

19. PRESENTATIONS ARE SUCCESSFUL THANKS TO THE PRE-PRESENTATION.

It's best not to surprise a client on the day of a presentation.

PRE-PRESENTATION

There is one thing to note about the Ranatunga Doctrine. It calls for delivering a deluge of insights and meaningful hypotheses. How does one do this when you only see the client once or twice a week at best, and you only see the CEO possibly once every week at the very best?

There are two ways:

> First, I tend to send very brief, frequent emails to Guillermo. They are short bursts of insightful information that we are finding. I am careful not to just send him data, but real insights.
>
> An example is when we found out why credit guarantees are not growing. I made an agreement with him about how to use this information. Typically, we would prefer not to send such information to the client so often since the client would not know how to use it and would overreact.
>
> So, Guillermo has agreed to check things with me before responding. forwarding, or adding it to executive meetings.
>
> Second, the notes we have been keeping for this book have turned out to be extremely useful for managing the client and team. I do not need to provide as many updates as I normally do since Guillermo can read and see what we are doing from the notes. The version he sees is, however, edited and excludes some information, such as team training, team concerns, thoughts on dealing with competitors, and more.

WEEK 1: INTERVIEWS AND ANALYSES

Remember, in consulting, we use pre-presentations, a.k.a. "pre-presents," before the client meeting. This is different from a simple alignment meeting.

Most firms set up senior client update meetings and, in those meetings, the client sees the material for the first time. Since the material is new, the client may struggle to understand it and, therefore, struggles to make a decision.

We use pre-presents to sit down with each client before the update, talk them through each slide, and when the actual update meeting occurs, they are able to make decisions since they already know all the details (from the pre-presents). Thus, this is not an update meeting, but a decision meeting.

Here's one interesting thing. The pre-presents are getting more interesting since the notes to create this book is turning into a sort of pre-present for the pre-present. So, we have a far more educated and in-tune client for the pre-presents and for the main update.

That is great and something we did not expect.

I get client emails quite often inquiring about things in the notes, and I then clarify or expand on that question through a new note.

PAUSE & REFLECT

> How could you incorporate pre-presents into your work, and what results would you aspire to achieve?

> Does your firm have a flexible approach and sufficiently large profit margin to use pre-presents?

> Can your firm afford to roll out the best practices you have been exposed to so far?

> How will you prioritize what best practices to implement?

WEEK 1: INTERVIEWS AND ANALYSES

STRATEGY

20. IT IS BEST TO WRAP UP FOCUS INTERVIEWS AND SHADOW STUDIES AS EARLY AS POSSIBLE.

What is the point of doing further analyses to prioritize, once you have the priorities?

FIELD NOTES

The team spent all of Saturday with field agents from the DFI. Field agents help mentor and follow up on delinquencies from borrowers. It was a fun day in torrid heat.

The agents mostly travel alone in cars. One or two use scooters, but these tend to be students who sometimes work as agents during the summer months. Those who have cars seem to have very nice vehicles. There is a disparity in that some of the things they use seem high end and other things seem quite cheap.

A typical agent is serving a 50- to 100-square-mile area. They can serve larger areas, but in this desert town, most of the action takes place in concentrated locations.

The agents try to see one borrower an hour, and work 10 hours a day, so they cover forty-five borrowers a week. Monday morning is spent in the office filing paperwork.

The agents have almost zero technology. Our agent was using a Nokia phone. Someone still has a Nokia phone! Agents are paid a base salary and a commission based on the profits their assigned borrower will generate.

Most profits are from penalties for late payments.

Most of the agents are women, since the DFI found it is easier for women to get meetings.

That said, some areas looked extremely dangerous and the agent pointed out she would only take us to the safer areas.

There is very little paperwork done in the field since the agents know what is happening and typically wrap up things at the end of the day.

The agents try to make appointments in advance, but if a borrower avoids them, they spring a surprise visit.

Due to the delays and so on, most of the visits involve waiting for the borrower.

If a borrower has delayed a payment, the agent offers to take them to an ABM to collect the outstanding payment in cash. The agent has a camera to record the transaction (the agents bought this with their own money to prevent allegations of fraud and abuse), though I am convinced this may be an abuse of the borrower's rights.

The agents seem to spend a lot of their own money on items, which probably indicates their salaries are larger than we were led to believe.

The work is very hard. The locations are difficult to find. It is hot, dry, and dusty. It could kill a lesser person.

The agents are very well trained at negotiating. They are non-confrontational, speak excellent English and Spanish, and are generally very pleasant to observe in action. They seem to care a lot.

Most agents are mothers and see this as a full-time, long-term career. They do not receive any benefits. That said, quite a few are on private medical schemes, which, again, indicates they are probably earning much more than we originally assumed.

Most of the branch employees, including the agents, are either direct or extended family of the DFI owner.

WEEK 1 WRAPS UP

I wonder how the agent model would work if loan applications were better screened up front? This is a very labor-intensive and low-tech process since the DFI is underinvesting in technology and exploiting the apparent low labor-cost advantage in the regions where it operates.

It's hard to imagine that 10% of the engagement is done, but we have done about 15% to 18% of the work. I think we have established a good foundation to move forward. It's time to plan the update scheduled for next week with Guillermo.

PAUSE & REFLECT

> Do you think there is a realistic business case to automate or digitize the key processes?

> What are the implications of only using female field agents?

> Which of our hypotheses can be tested with the information above?

STRATEGY

WEEK 2 / PART 1

---

3 *days*

LESSONS IN GREAT MANAGEMENT, CASE STUDIES AND FOCUS INTERVIEWS WRAP UP, LESSONS IN CONFIDENCE BUILDING AND WORKING TOGETHER, PREPARING FOR THE FIRST EXECUTIVE UPDATE MEETING WITH THE CLIENT, ANALYSES AND REPORTS FOR THE CEO AND CFO.

SECOND INTERNAL UPDATE MEETING

week 2 / part 1: INTERVIEWS, STUDIES, MEETINGS

1. FORCE THE MANAGER TO STEP INTO THE LEADERSHIP ROLE.

Asking is usually not enough to bring out the best in people.

RECAP OF WEEK 1

We had three successes in the last week:

1. Good start to the engagement in Week 1
2. Developing critical and counterintuitive insights
3. Instilling confidence in the client that our thinking and analysis is rigorous and will not be another engagement to rubber-stamp the client's ideas

Given this, I am going to think carefully about what needs to be shown in the first update. Since the client already knows we have produced some unique insights, we do not need to show everything at once.

We will show it once the story is clearer.

So, the agenda for the first update will be:

1. Review of LAB's financials (top-down financial analyses)
2. Our revised approach

I think the results of the LAB financial analyses will be enough to demonstrate we need a change to the study.

But the focus will be on our revised approach and there I want to discuss:

1. The time lines
2. Market-entry decision framework**
3. The engagement approach
4. Focus interviews list
5. DFI shadow studies list
6. Case study list
7. Financial model architecture
8. Critical issues we must address**
9. Overview of the options**
10. Timing for the engagement

Items with a double asterisk are the key ones for the CEO. The rest are for Guillermo.

Notice that we don't produce raw data just to show the client we have done eighty shadow studies, twenty interviews, and more. That adds little value. We will only present the insights from this work once we have figured out the insights and their implications.

We don't want to present an insight where we don't understand the implications. Why? Because the client could end up interpreting the insight in a way that takes the engagement in a direction, we don't believe is right.

It's similar to the advice young trial lawyers are given; don't ask a question to which you do not know the answer. For us, the answer is the implication.

The critical issues slide is useful. Our original hypothesis was that we would find the retail structure to be a capital destroyer. Now we are adding credit guarantees to that because everything seems to point in that direction, but we need more numbers to corroborate this.

We will then need to think about other ways for LAB to fulfill its mandate.

This is not the result LAB expects, but I suspect it will turn out this way.

For those of you reading this and worried about understanding terms like capital destruction, please do not worry overly about this. There are many technical ways to think of capital; just assume that is all the cash the company has to loan to the market.

Sometimes we call this a fund. That capital grows as a loan is made, and the loan is repaid with the interest. The capital shrinks if a loan defaults and all the costs associated with managing the business that will eat up the capital.

It is not a precise definition, but it's enough to really understand this engagement and develop all the analyses and insights.

Later, we will probably have to discuss the balance sheet and risk, but that's also not as scary as it seems if you don't have a business or finance background.

Think of the balance sheet as that place in your house where you hide the documentation for everything valuable. It's like a big safe or storage area of everything you own and all the loan documents for money you owe people and banks.

STRATEGY

So, when we talk about a risk to your balance sheet, we don't really mean someone is going to damage this storage area.

We mean that something valuable, like your home whose deed is in the storage area, may be damaged.

A balance sheet is just a list. We are worried about what will happen to the things listed on the balance sheet. If you think about a balance sheet this way, the study will be much easier to follow.

None of us have a development finance background on this team, and we are doing just fine. You are in good company.

A KEY SLIDE

These are some of the critical issues that I think the CEO and I will spend discussing for about 90% of the executive meeting. There will be just one slide about this.

1. What happens if the direct-entry US retail option is not feasible?
2. Is there potential to grow through any existing channels?
3. Are there any other key market segments not being addressed by LAB?
4. Which segments are other government institutions and other intermediaries addressing?
5. How quickly and efficiently can different DFI options be scaled to extend loans?
6. What potential for conflict exists if LAB does decide to enter the market directly?

7. Are there any legal constraints that need to be addressed if LAB enters the market directly, for instance, anti-competition law if acquisition is selected, additional Treasury requirements, US-Mexican banking agreements?

8. Does LAB have the capabilities, skills, and capacity to enter the market and run DFIs directly?

GUIDING ALBERT

Today will be a long day with Albert as he talks me through his approach to analyzing the economics of the retail branch network.

I will be looking for specific output in this meeting to help me understand if Albert is on the right path. I will need:

1. The objective of the model
2. Single-page model description
3. Drivers and levers of capital appreciation (a fancy way of saying, Does LAB have more or less cash over time)
4. Model architecture
5. Assumptions and approach to model demand
6. Assumptions and approach to modeling the loan book and default rate
7. If he is going to do this state by state, aggregating the data into regions or focusing on a few critical states?

My expectation is that Albert will be done with the planning but possibly want my guidance to round out some areas. I am also interested to see if he can simplify complex analyses, or will he try to build the model that answers everything.

We will spend the entire day together, and you will find that we build models like nothing you have seen or read about anywhere before.

TRAINING AN ENGAGEMENT MANAGER

Nimisha has the toughest role. There is no doubt about that.

She has no consulting experience, and the team knows that. Not only must she learn technical skills at a faster rate than the rest of the team, but she also needs to learn and deploy additional skills to manage the team.

The associates will question her judgment because they know she knows as little as they do.

Yet she has done tremendously well—far better than expected—and she is at the point where she basically manages the team by herself.

This does not just happen.

Most partners will only let a manager take charge if she has the respect of the team and the knowledge. Yet a manager can only get the respect of the team and gain the knowledge if she takes charge or went to some incredible school or worked at a major firm that her team thought was impressive.

So, it is a chicken-and-egg problem.

Nimisha took the advice and was very effective at establishing and building cohesion in the team, as well as using the governance structure to communicate up and down the team.

We did a few things that allowed Nimisha become the de facto leader quickly:

Leave Nimisha alone. Even though I am spending a lot of time on the engagement site, I am not working 100% on the engagement. I have a room within the engagement room, and I can work on other initiatives. I also spend time away from the team when I am working on the engagement simply planning and training clients.

In this way, I am not smothering Nimisha. I am forcing the team to go to her for management decisions versus coming to me, merely because I am there.

Make real decisions independently. If Nimisha were frequently calling or texting me for advice, the team would see this and realize she was not the real leader. They would realize she was merely the mouthpiece of the engagement leader.

So, I sent the team to New Mexico alone and basically told Nimisha she was alone: Only contact me for something urgent, I told her. Not everything went smoothly in New Mexico, but when the team saw Nimisha making decisions without my input, they realized she was acting as the leader, and ergo, was the leader.

Understand that a great manager does not have to know everything. A manager does not need to have technical mastery. Albert, for example, will typically know more about the economics of the retail structure since that is the area he owns.

Nimisha can still guide him because Nimisha, and not Albert, knows more about what is happening on the other streams and, therefore, what is needed from Albert's stream to bring together the entire engagement.

I also trained her how to think through issues when she is not an expert in them. The key is to ask the right questions. In this way, Nimisha is confident in her abilities to ask questions when she is not the technical expert because she will not be the technical expert under most circumstances.

Delegate. I force myself not to do things that I could do in three minutes, if it is not a partner role. It may take Nimisha twenty minutes to do it, and it will cost us more in time, but over the ten weeks she will get faster and this frees up my time to work on "thinking stuff."

Never coach and mentor Nimisha in front of the associates. That would simply undermine her. I mentor her when she is alone or when we can speak on the phone privately. To save time, most partners save up training issues, but this hurts the manager.

I changed Nimisha's attire. I made her dress in a more conservative but stylish manner. She had to tailor just about everything because she is tall and lithe. The way you dress matters enormously. I made her dress in a more professional and preppy manner.

Finally, Nimisha has also been very effective at communicating with and managing the client. She has mastered the situation-specific leadership approach very quickly. I noticed she uses different approaches even with Peter and Alex.

Situation-specific leadership is a central concept we teach management consultants, and I am pleased to see her pick this up so quickly.

PAUSE & REFLECT

> Why do you think you were probably more interested in the financial analyses exhibits than how Nimisha grew as a leader?

> What does this mean for your career development and what you value as a professional?

> Why do you think we selected those questions for the CEO?

> What is the best outcome we are seeking when discussing those questions with the CEO?

STRATEGY

2. DON'T LET THE BUSINESS CASE ANALYSES BEGIN UNLESS THE PLANNING IS CRYSTAL CLEAR.

"Build the model and everything will work" is not a strategy.

STRUCTURING THE BUSINESS CASE

I am going to provide a rundown of some of the key points we discussed during Albert's planning meeting.

> We are going to model demand. The decision has been made. That means we need to find a way to calculate how the demand for loans through the DFIs will change by state, by loan size and by the sector where the borrower's business is based.

> We have to model this demand by state since each state is different, and we may even group states to create zones like a Pacific South Zone.

> We have to find a way to estimate the number of registered and unregistered small businesses in the US and calculate the percentage LAB can realistically capture.

> The key thing is being able to forecast the growth in new businesses set up and the percentage of businesses LAB will fund.

We have ways to do that and I believe we can be reasonably accurate. Accuracy, though, is less valuable than knowing the economics. This is how Albert and I talked this out:

STRATEGY

Albert: I think we should model twenty-eight segments of borrowers.

Partner: That's 28 x 10 x 9 x 4 x 9 discrete groups that must be analyzed. I do not think that helps us understand the economics of the DFIs. We are not here to understand the borrowing segments.

A: How did you get that?

P: That's twenty-eight borrower segments that must be split by different interest-rate ranges, different sectors, repayment periods, and different states.

A: I did not think about that.

P: Have you ever seen a financial model with twenty-eight segments?

A: No, but I think it makes sense here.

P: Why?

A: The twenty-eight segments are different. They behave differently.

P: Fair enough. So how did you arrive at twenty-eight segments? Why not model thirty-eight or sixty-eight segments?

A: That's too much.

P: How do you know twenty-eight is not too much?

A: It seems manageable. I think I can do that.

P: Your main criterion for selecting segments should not be your ability to manage your workload. You need to group segments that will apply for the same loan sizes. So single fathers, single mothers, etc., are different in the way they behave. But you should group borrowers by the loan sizes they will pursue. Nothing else really matters.

A: Yes, that makes sense to me.

ESTIMATING THE NUMBER OF BRANCHES AND PROFITS

Once we know the demand, and by using the current DFI branch ratios, we can reasonably estimate how many branches LAB will need to cater to that demand, and where and when they would need to build them all.

So, in effect, what is the capital expenditure sequence?

That CAPEX (capital expenditures), along with the OPEX (operating expenses) of running the branches, which we can estimate with a high degree of accuracy after spending last week in New Mexico analyzing the branches, allows us to see the cost incurred to manage the volume we can expect.

We can, thereafter, determine what combination of the following generates the most profits:

1. Loan sizes
2. Interest rates
3. Repayment periods
4. Location of branches (by state and urban versus rural sites)

STRATEGY

Finally, once we know that optimal combination, we can determine if LAB can realistically achieve those targets.

We need to play around with the numbers to test sensitivities.

> First, let's keep everything constant but play around with the volume of loans served. At what volume do we break even? Is it realistic to think we can achieve that volume?
>
> If realistic, do we have the capital to pursue that realistic volume?
>
> Next, we hold the volume of loans constant (or at a constant growth rate) but play around with the mix of loans. What if 90% of the loans are for $5,000? What if 90% are for $35,000? We want to see what mix is most profitable and if there is a loan size LAB cannot serve because it is unprofitable to serve.
>
> We can play around with interest rates as well. What if we offered very competitive interest rates? How would LAB's profits, capital appreciation and pay-back-period change?
>
> We can add mentors to the program and estimate the change in variable costs and profits?
>
> We also have to estimate the default rate and work out how LAB will need to allow for that on their balance sheet as a reserve. This one will be tricky, but I think the aim is to see if LAB can be profitable with its current default rate and then see if it's current customer mix will match its new customer mix. If not, do we increase or decrease the default rate and by how much?
>
> Credit guarantees are an entirely different issue.

CREDIT GUARANTEES DO NOT FALL INTO OUR SCOPE OF WORK

That said, our working hypothesis is that LAB would not be able to profitably build a retail branch network in the US, due to the high operating costs and low volumes. Therefore, it would need to focus more on restructuring the bank's current products and building better relationships with the DFIs and retail banks.

If that is true, I can almost see a break point in this engagement. Once we are done with the economics of the retail channel, we need to think of how LAB achieves its mandate with a retail partner, without entering the US market.

That is a finding no one expects, but we have to be open to that possibility. It is highly unlikely that the retail economics would be so good that we will be planning a pilot rollout in eight weeks.

If that happens, I will be shocked because the numbers do not intuitively add up so far.

Therefore, the break point in the engagement would be showing that the retail structure is uneconomical and shifting the engagement to fix the current products to make them profitable within the current structure. This is how credit guarantees become part of the engagement.

THE MODEL ARCHITECTURE

Here in **Exhibit 22** is the blueprint that I will analyze in extensive detail before giving Albert permission to proceed.

STRATEGY

EXHIBIT 22: Financial model architecture

A logical framework is used to build the business model with a 10-year time horizon

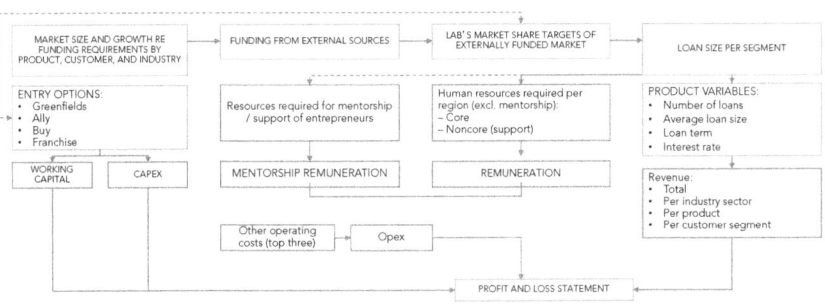

We spent 97 minutes discussing the slide block by block and ensuring the analyses were being conducted correctly. In any business case analysis with a model, this is one of the three most important planning documents.

I will look at this a few times, think about whether the logic is there, and consider the best way to accomplish each task. That said, from today, Albert will know more than me about this since the content is closer to him.

However, I still know the right questions to ask to test his thinking, because as a strategy partner, I am trained to understand how to unpack and repackage business models.

Don't worry about VLOOKUPs. You do not need any of that to build an effective financial model. As long as it works, it does not need to be fancy.

PAUSE & REFLECT

> How do you currently plan your financial modeling?
> Can you recall the differences between financial analysis and financial modeling and when each is used on a strategy engagement?
> What would we have received if we had asked Albert to build a financial model and provided little guidance?
> What would you do in the first five days after you had been told to build a financial model?

STRATEGY

3. CASE STUDIES ARE HARD WORK, REQUIRING EXTENSIVE CORROBORATION.

They should not be the easiest part of the engagement.

CASE STUDIES

I spent the last forty-five minutes talking Peter through the questions I would want answered from the first case study. We do not do the same analyses for every case study since each case is trying to teach us something different.

The mistake, a very common one with consultants, is to create a process to make every case study look the same. That serves no purpose.

I will focus on carefully choosing each case study to provide guidance, data, and benchmarks for a hypothesis we are trying to answer for LAB.

For the first case study, it is about how they instituted their turnaround and whether it was successful. The literature says it was successful, but the literature is routinely wrong, so we want data from the company to verify that the turnaround was successful by serving the low end of the market.

If it was achieved by cross subsidies, then this supports our contention that some segments are unattractive to serve.

FOCUS INTERVIEWS AND SHADOW STUDIES ARE ENDING

By the end of the day tomorrow, we will have finished thirty focus interviews with industry stakeholders, two DFI shadow studies, and we expect about ninety-five to 105 shadow studies of entrepreneurs.

More is not necessarily better since we feel the focus interviews have already played a major role in pointing out a few new issues and helping us understand some areas we were not clear about.

Here is an insight: One well-crafted focus interview can generate more value than twenty

rushed, poorly structured, and poorly prepared focus interviews.

Of the one hundred or so entrepreneur day-in-the-life-of shadow studies completed, our readers and clients did eighty-one. A big thank you to everyone who took the time to help us.

What did we want with the one hundred immigrant shadow studies?

To create a graph. Just one graph.

We wanted to create a pie graph of the time spent on value-adding and non-value-adding work. We wanted to see if there was a business case for reducing time spent on non-value work, like traveling to a bank.

That will be a key insight for us.

WEDNESDAY SESSION

On Wednesday afternoon, we plan to put up onto the office walls all the following slides and spend time thinking about what it all means:

1. Focus interview summary slides
2. Shadow engagement of immigrants summary slides
3. Shadow engagement of DFI summary slides
4. Top-down financial analyses
5. Early case study output

This is similar to those FBI profiling shows where the agents put all key information on a wall and search for the linkages and cause and effect.

We work in the opposite direction. We have the cause and effect via the decision trees. We also have the hypotheses.

We are searching for the data to prove or disprove our hypotheses.

Tomorrow is another fairly hectic day where we are tying up lots of the top-down analyses. Once the ink settles on that, we can step back and think about the likely direction the engagement will take.

The working hypothesis remains that the US retail market is not viable for our banking client, and credit guarantees are a sinkhole. Now we just have to prove it and prove it conclusively, not with erroneous and superficial anecdotes.

By the way, the other consulting firm and the internal strategy group have finally asked for a meeting. You should treat everyone with the utmost respect and professionalism. You are the way you act.

We plan to speak to them on Friday afternoon to answer the questions they have and to be helpful. The client does not benefit in turf wars, and we need to place the clients' interests first at all times. I firmly believe that the quality of our work alone will earn our right to continue serving the CEO.

STRATEGY

PAUSE & REFLECT

> Could we have done anything to improve the case studies?

> Do you see the rigorous approach to using data in order to test the hypotheses and storyboard?

> What would have happened if we conducted analyses that were not driven by the hypotheses?

WEEK 2 / PART 1: INTERVIEWS, STUDIES, MEETINGS

4. LEARN HOW TO GET THINGS DONE WITH LOW CONFIDENCE.

Gaining confidence does not imply you can get the job done.

PETER

I am up early today to lead the focus interview with a former senior financial executive who worked with the first case company studied during the alleged financial turnaround of the business.

I would have left this to Peter, but I have not actually seen him in action and these focus interviews could be slightly problematic.

So, I will join him for at least the first twenty-one, let him see how to manage things by observing me, and then hand it over to him.

Peter is a very quiet but an extremely capable consultant. I like that quality. He does not talk a lot about his capabilities but asks questions, is thoughtful, and is very meticulous about meeting the standards we set.

His slides are unbelievably good—when he knows they will be used.

He takes a lot of care to get things right, and I am usually surprised about the quality and volume he produces. I wonder if he will be able to keep up such high standards in the future.

I personally enjoy working with him.

CONFIDENCE, A TRICKY SUBJECT

Confidence invariably comes up during internship mentoring, but not in the way you think.

In our onboarding and strategy training, we are careful not to discuss it.

Confidence is a lot like profits. You do not discuss profits, but you discuss all the things needed, like good products, customer service, etc., which will ultimately lead to profits.

That is one reason we do not discuss it. We focus on teaching the interns such a strong approach to solving problems that if they just trust the way we do things, they will be fine.

At first, they were skeptical, but by now, they can see the impact of the approach. They believe in the process.

There is another reason we do not teach confidence.

It is a myth that you need to be confident to succeed. That is something taught by business schools and self-help gurus to tap into our inner anxiety and sell us things we do not need—mainly books on how to build confidence.

Here is the most striking thing about self-development. If you have confidence in a technical skill, then you are not really growing as a person.

Here is a more interesting point, even if you were technically gifted. If your life was structured in such a way that your husband or wife made you feel like a loser, you would still lack confidence at the office since we cannot conveniently separate the two.

So, confidence is this very tricky thing that seems to be built on technical skills, but not really.

We like to think it is built on technical skills since that makes us feel good. Having technical skills makes us feel that we have more control over confidence.

We take a very different approach to confidence.

We believe you do not need confidence to do a great job. Confidence is how you feel when you accomplish something.

That is a major point. It is not the act of accomplishing something.

Do you feel great when you accomplish something or just plain lousy?

Does it really matter? You accomplished it right?

We often say that you rarely really gain confidence. You merely learn to accept the state of confidence you have.

But you can accomplish astonishing things with the level that you do have.

People think I have lots of confidence, but I probably have less confidence than many others. I just do things. Lots of times, I will challenge a client, not because I have confidence. I do it because that is why I was hired, to ensure the best idea gets airtime.

Next time you worry that your lack of confidence is holding you back, think about this: Irrespective of how you feel, and confidence is a feeling, you have a job to do and you need to do it.

Unless your contract says you can underperform when your confidence is low, you have to deliver.

DEMONSTRATED CONFIDENCE

One thing I taught Nimisha is not to worry about her school. I pointed out that the team and potentially clients would look at her non-Ivy background and give her a hard time. She should not worry.

This is not true, but she does not need to know this. There are times when something needs to be withheld.

If she develops a style of consistently demonstrating why she is right, she will take longer to develop respect, but she will earn a deeper respect and a more sustainable type of leadership.

So many people get intimidated when they hear the words, Baker scholar and Rhodes scholar. The trick is not to enter the conversation and try to win by seeing who flashes the most sparkly credentials.

It is best to incrementally gain respect because you are right, and you care.

If you have an allegedly weaker brand-name school, the solution is demonstrated confidence.

Let me give you an example of this.

In the first update Albert had with Nimisha, I was within earshot. Albert started off by explaining how he had used his experience building models for company X and company Y, winning this and that award.

Albert was flashing his credentials and hoping that would be a proxy for his intellect so that Nimisha would not analyze his work.

Albert was basically saying, "I have done this before, so trust me."

Nimisha was trained to politely thank him for that but focus on the actual work done.

She focused on the objective function of the model:

STRATEGY

1. What would its outputs be?
2. What would it not do? Why?
3. What were the key assumptions? Why?
4. What were the variables? Why?
5. What scenarios and options could be analyzed?

You could clearly see this put Albert off his game. Why is this?

Albert had not been trained to demonstrate his competency on a daily basis. Albert was someone who had gotten away with flashing his credentials and had neglected the skill of demonstrating he knew what he should have known.

It's not that he is not competent, but rather that he was rarely challenged due to his academic credentials and work experience.

Therefore, he does not need to try as hard. And, therefore, his work quality slides at times.

The dynamic in that relationship changed pretty fast—right in front of my eyes—because Albert realized Nimisha was not someone who was going to be pushed aside by credentials.

Remember, doing a good job comes from two things: being intellectually curious and doing the work. Plenty of intellectual people don't put in the effort.

Plenty of people go to brand-name schools and do not need to prove themselves, and hence, lose this capability. Just as an Olympic athlete who doesn't train, the flab eventually sets in.

Even if someone went to the best school you could imagine and they were smart, it does not mean they'd work as hard to uncover an insight. That casualness implies the insight is not as helpful as it could have been.

So be wary of assuming people who graduate from brand-name schools have smart insights. Brand-name graduates, like the graduates of any school, sometimes tend to coast on their brands and believe they have earned the right to work a little less.

That is when you can exploit this difference.

And I can assure you, even if a Nobel Prize winner were in front of me, I would not assume he or she was right. That is the way I was trained, and that is the way a great consultant engages with issues. I would be eminently respectful, but it is my job to check the facts and logic for myself.

A smart person who works hard consistently and demonstrates competency in each interaction is pretty much unstoppable, even if that person did not attend a great school.

STRATEGY

PAUSE & REFLECT

> How do you react when someone with impressive credentials challenges you?

> How could your career and life improve if you did things without waiting for a feeling, a.k.a. confidence, to arrive?

> How can you ensure that you proceed with a task, especially when you lack confidence?

… WEEK 2 / PART 1: INTERVIEWS, STUDIES, MEETINGS

STRATEGY

5. IF LAB WILL BE IMMENSELY PROFITABLE IN TWENTY YEARS, WE WOULD HAVE FAILED.

LAB exists due to a broken system, and its existence implies the system remains broken

BROKEN SYSTEM VS. BITTER PARTICIPANT

Last night, I was talking to a client about his pending direct-partner entry interviews at BCG and McKinsey, and I made the following distinction.

He pointed out that he was not happy he did not go to a great school and that he felt intimidated when he interviewed with the partners at major firms. He implied that it was unfair.

He knew he was just as good, but he felt he was in the back seat and had to prove himself constantly.

I made this telling distinction:

> "Are you unhappy because the system we have places too much emphasis on an Ivy League degree, or are you happy with the system but unhappy you did not benefit from this system? They are entirely different issues."

It was a revelation for him to think this way. And it is a revelation for most people to think this way.

Most times, we are not unhappy with an imperfect system, which we know is imperfect. Rather, we are unhappy that we did not benefit from that system. You see that all the time. When people complain about a system, be it wages or access to services, they are not looking to change a bad system, but just trying to make sure they benefit from it.

If they did, even if they knew it was an unfair system, they would not change it.

Why is this mentioned? Because one of the major styles of thinking I am trying to get the team to learn is the following:

> "Is the current model of development finance a broken system, or is the system correct but poorly implemented?"

The first time I was exposed to this style of thinking is when I read these words in Nelson Mandela's trial transcripts.

It is quite powerful:

> "The complaint of Africans, however, is not only that they are poor and that whites are rich, but also that the laws, which are designed by whites, are designed to preserve this situation."
>
> There are two ways to break out of poverty. The first is through formal education, and the second is through the worker acquiring a greater skill at his work and, thus, higher wages. As far as Africans are concerned, both of these avenues of advancement are deliberately curtailed by legislation.
>
> The current government has sought to hamper Africans in their search for education. One of the government's early acts, after coming into power, was to stop subsidies for free meals in African schools. Many African children who attended schools depended on this supplement to their diet. This was a cruel act.
>
> There is compulsory education for all white children at virtually no cost to their parents, be they rich or poor. Similar facilities

are not provided to the African children, though there are some who receive such assistance. African children, however, generally have to pay more for their schooling than whites."

The striking thing about this speech is that you could basically change "whites" and "Africans" for other races and ethnicities, and it would be universally relevant.

We are focusing on the second part Mandela raises, about giving workers greater skills and higher wages.

Mandela's defense is the modern declaration of independence. It is the context-heavy version of the Abraham Lincoln speech. It is a universal Magna Carta.

It is a manifesto for why development finance is, actually, a terrible industry that should not exist.

Development finance was basically created because bad government policies disenfranchise so many, and microfinance is the apparent solution when the government has failed.

In other words, do we celebrate LAB meeting its mandate or bemoan the fact that LAB had to be created in the first place to fund survivalist businesses? That is a deeper question.

Our job is, therefore, to make LAB so successful that it is no longer needed in twenty years. That is the true measure of success in this engagement.

If in twenty years, LAB is still here, immensely profitable and a well-managed and efficient organization, then we have failed miserably.

PAUSE & REFLECT

> Should the smartest minds join a well-meaning government organization that exists to plug a hole created by the failure of said government?

> Or should they join said government to fix the problem at its root, thereby negating the need for the well-meaning government organization?

> Or should they join the private sector, which is trying to sustainably correct the failure?

STRATEGY

6. COMMITMENT IS MORE IMPORTANT THAN INTELLECT.

If you are committed, you will get the job done.

COMMITMENT VS. INTELLECT

Everything I know about strategy, I can eventually teach you, the same way that one of the firm's youngest partners taught me a lot of things he knew.

I discuss this extensively in "Partnership. Memoir[38], (Re)Building a Consulting Practice[39] and Mapping a Strategy Partner's Career[40]."

I cannot teach you to be trustworthy or committed. You gain those from life experiences. You either have them or you don't.

And I really don't want someone learning to be committed and trustworthy, for the first time, at the expense of a client.

Most people who want a chance at a firm like BCG, and Bain will claim to be committed. They say they just need a chance to prove themselves.

What is missing is the evidence that they are committed and trustworthy.

---

[38] http://www.strategytraining.com/partner-memoir-from-ba-to-director-before-age-30

[39] https://www.strategytraining.com/rebuilding-a-consulting-practice

[40] https://www.strategytraining.com/analyzing-a-strategy-partner-s-career

STRATEGY

We have this commitment fetish such that we think everyone wants to know how committed we are. It is incredibly hard to show and is best demonstrated. If you ever have to resort to telling anyone you are committed, then you have failed to prove it.

Here is a good example.

Peter was up all night preparing his slides and preparing for the focus interview. He did not tell me about this when I went in this morning. I just assumed he had arrived early. The security at the front desk told me a few minutes ago that Peter had been in the office all night.

His work is done now. And it looks good.

That is commitment.

He did not tell us he was committed.

The commitment was not the output.

The commitment was the input, and his work was the output. The result speaks for themselves.

Contrast his behavior with an employee who focuses on the hours worked and makes sure everyone knows about their sacrificed time, while ignoring the value they created in that time.

This is what most employees do. They want to be rewarded for the hours worked, even if the output is mediocre.

An employee working longer hours while generating incrementally lower output is a drain on productivity. If they are paid higher overtime wages, they are increasing costs.

Do not turn commitment into a Valentine's Day stunt: treating your partner like a disposable razor for the majority of the year, then buying roses, chocolates, and a dinner to show your commitment on just one day.

Show it throughout the year on the little things.

HERE IS A BRIEF RECAP OF THE DAY

I think some fatigue is setting into the team. They did not have much of a weekend, and we had a hard two days of the week already where we were building up to essentially three important update meetings: Guillermo, CEO, and the other consulting firm. I will talk about the strategy we are using after the meeting with a rival firm.

Thirty focus interviews were done and were incredibly useful. As I said before, if you are doing a strategy engagement or any engagement for that matter without focus interviews, I would be worried.

We finished 107 immigrant shadow studies, and I believe two more are still to come in from Rhode Island and Hawaii. That is a lot of work to produce just two exhibits to test two crucial hypotheses.

The write-ups from the DFI shadow studies in New Mexico are done. They are very interesting as well.

The first draft of the detailed first case study is done. It is a period case study, which means it is examining a period in the bank's history and that made the case hard to complete.

Most of yesterday was spent on the phone helping Peter either conduct focus interviews, adjust his questions or help him find and review data. We finished that around 11 p.m.; remember the bank we studied is in a time zone that's ahead of us.

Now that Peter observed how I managed the first case, I am sure he will be able to do the rest better, though both Nimisha and I will support as needed.

The top-down financial analyses are done, checked, and approved.

So that was the day. We hit our internal target and have another tough but great day ahead of us.

PAUSE & REFLECT

> How do you demonstrate your commitment?

> Should you measure the hours worked and effort made versus the output value you created?

> Do you get upset when your manager is not appreciative of the long hours you put in, even if your output is weak?

> What can you do to be more output-value driven?

WEEK 2 / PART 1: INTERVIEWS, STUDIES, MEETINGS

7. THE REAL ACTION BEGINS WHEN THE ANALYSES ARE DONE.

You get to think about the implications and insights.

THE DAY AFTER THE ANALYSES

Most aspiring strategy consultants worry about the analyses. However, what happens when the analyses are done? That is when the actual strategy thinking takes place.

There must be a series of internal-only workshops where we look at all the analyses and think about the implications.

No two engagements are the same. Normally this step to pull everything together will occur later in the study. Here are some adjustments being made for this engagement, since we are just eight days into a fifty-day engagement:

1. We are not expecting stream storyboards or stream updates to be presented at this stage. The streams have not even started, so that is premature.

2. The stream storyboards should have been completed on Day 1, but they probably have not been updated them since then.

3. We will present updates on the major analyses done but not split them into streams.

4. The overall storyboard will be very short since only the top-down financial analysis is being presented. No more than five to eight slides.

5. A lot of time will be given to explaining the approach we are using. Generally, we would not do this, but given that other parts of the organization are clamoring to enter the market, we feel it is wise that the client understand why we are taking the approach we are taking.

6. We almost certainly are not going to recommend an option now, though we have some good hypotheses about which option we will eventually recommend.

7. Big difference here: We will not show anything from the focus interviews and shadow studies since we are not entirely clear yet what the insight is and how it impacts the client. Moreover, no one cares how many case studies we did. What matters is the insight we generated.

The value of this day is bringing everything we have discovered together in one place and thinking about what it means.

It is about assembling what we found, assimilating it into our approach, and seeing where that takes us. Of course, we have many strong hypotheses, but the data needs to take us there as well, or our hypotheses are wrong.

We need to go back to the original problem statement and determine if it remains valid. And if it is, are we still solving the original problem or are we deviating. And if we are staying focused, are we running the engagement in the most efficient manner.

WORD OF WARNING

There is no checklist or 1-29 steps that you must follow for a strategy engagement. The general approach is approximately the same, but the analysis will be different for each client. And even within the general approach, modifications may be needed.

Strategy is not a linear process.

There are processes, which we point out, but they need to be adjusted and altered based on the clients' needs.

That said, we apply core tools and techniques, but applying them by itself will not lead to a strategy.

For example, just being MECE (mutually exclusive and collectively exhaustive) or building a hypothesis is not going to save any client.

More, much more is required. Clients do not pay millions of dollars for an answer that can be found on Google, a textbook, or a report from another consulting firm. They expect real insights and real value that they can measure in their bank accounts.

Unfortunately, this is something that is best passed down by observing a real engagement in action. Like this book.

PAUSE & REFLECT

> How do you keep updated on the big picture in your own engagements?
> How do you define the big picture?[41]
> Why don't we expect the analyses to provide the answers?
> Why do we have to question the analyses first to arrive at a recommendation?

---

[41] https://www.firmsconsulting.com/podcasts/big-picture-thinking/

STRATEGY

8. NIMISHA USED CLEVER TECHNIQUES TO ASSUME LEADERSHIP.

They should be adopted by most consultants.

NIMISHA'S LEADERSHIP

It took me some time to figure out how Nimisha took control of the team so quickly. This is what I think she has been doing.

She almost exactly mirrors the tactics we are using to manage the client: less talking and more insights, and the principle of demonstrated competency. She basically does key things with the client and with the team that we are teaching. She watches what we do with the client and repeats it in managing the team. That is smart, not perfect, but smart.

Nimisha does not fall for the content trap. Nimisha is not trying to be the expert in everything Albert or Peter does. She is comfortable asking questions on topics they know better than she does.

She serves many times as a super-administrator. She is frequently on the phone with Guillermo's executive assistant, making sure things planned for the day take place as planned. She is clearing the way for the team to succeed. Engagement managers sometimes need to serve this role, and she does it well.

Unsexy work is done. Strategy consulting requires a lot of unsexy work that is indispensable, but no one wants to do it since it is so operational. She does it, if it helps the team, and still gets her work done. That is a good example of sacrificing herself for the team. Some of the associates like Albert will not do certain things because it is not "strategy consulting."

STRATEGY

Nimisha is learning to tie the pieces of data together. That is the main role of the engagement manager. As a new analysis is done, she sends me a short email with the implications. We find that incredibly useful. After focus interviews, she does not give me a one-page summary but a three-line summary of the things that are key to the engagement. That is also very useful.

She gets out of the way. Nimisha is not a bottleneck. She does not seem worried if the team bypasses her and comes to me directly for things. That is fairly normal and happens in an engagement. She pops up when she is needed but is essentially giving the team the room to maneuver.

Nimisha may be the one person who watched every video in A Typical McKinsey, BCG et al., Engagement[42] on StrategyTraining.com, even though I assumed she had not. Every tip we have suggested, including how to send emails to me, leave voice messages, ask for advice, send me slides, manage the client etc., she is following. I would not be surprised if she had a color-coded binder with a summary of all the tips.

She does not panic. When things go wrong, she is fairly calm and that helps the team. She also does not make excuses and does not waste time fumbling around to pull up old emails to see what was agreed. Anyone doing that is merely covering himself or herself. She merely focuses on solving the problem.

For someone with an accounting background, she is not obsessed with trying to show value by becoming too involved in the minutiae of the model. We see her leaving lots of Post-it notes on Albert's issue map, but that is about it. That is a good sign since many graduates

---

[42] https://www.strategytraining.com/follow-a-full-mckinsey-et-al-engagement

with technical degrees tend to be obsessed with using their technical skills and often miss the broader pattern.

She does not draw attention to her differences. She does not consume alcohol nor eat meat. When the team goes out and people want wine, she does not make a big deal when the waiter brings her meat or wine. She just quietly avoids it. I have seen her eat celery during an entire dinner. That is very smart. It is best not to draw attention to your differences. In fact, she does not draw attention to herself. She draws attention to the engagement, so you do not really learn much about her. Which is also very clever.

Nimisha does not criticize anything. She had nothing negative to say about anyone, any sports team, or anyone's choices. This way, she does not make enemies.

Of course, she has weaknesses like everyone else, but we should give credit where it is due: As an Indian woman coming from a school with a weaker brand than the team's, she is managing and working for a client with very few female managers, and she is doing very well.

PAUSE & REFLECT

> What changes can you make to your leadership style by next week to achieve similar results to Nimisha's?

> Do you wait to be asked to lead?

> When do you choose to lead?

> How do you define leadership[43]

---

[43] https://www.firmsconsulting.com/podcasts/talk-about-a-leadership-example-sample-answer/

WEEK 2 / PART 1: INTERVIEWS, STUDIES, MEETINGS

STRATEGY

9. THIS ENGAGEMENT MATTERS TO THE US, WHICH MANAGES SEVERAL LARGE STATE BANKS.

Deciding their strategies is a continuous debate.

STATE-OWNED BANKS IN THE US

This was discussed quite a bit in our morning team meeting so that the team could understand the broader strategy issues at play.

Earlier I mentioned that one of the issues facing LAB, which is capitalized by a national government, is understanding its role relative to the private sector. In a nutshell, why should LAB enter attractive market segments if, by virtue of their attractive returns, those banking segments would attract private sector-investors?

In most cases, it should not.

Therefore, we raised the point that LAB would be forced to enter segments so unattractive that they would make no returns. And due to this, they would need to enter an attractive market outside Mexico and Latin America, to subsidize their losses in Latin America.

You can look at it this way. If it costs $1 billion for LAB to enter an attractive market segment in Mexico, that is $1 billion less that LAB has to spend in an unattractive market segment in Mexico that's not getting any private-sector investment.

Obviously, LAB should be in the unattractive segment in Mexico, but it needs to find ways to subsidize those losses.

If the US government is not involved in the US financial services sector, should a bank backed by a foreign government be involved?

Yes, because it frees the US government to spend capital on other, more pressing issues.

So, LAB need not worry about this.

TEAM MEETING

The internal update meetings are very useful, and we use a set, visually striking format and template[44] to present.

That was a short, sharp, and great meeting. The team has momentum, and we plan to finish this week in a big way, pushing heavily into the case studies and understanding the economics of the retail branch network.

I want insights to fall like rain in the Amazon jungle in a summer storm—without the mosquitoes, of course.

We're off to spend quality time with Albert and see what he has done on the business-case side.

---

[44] https://www.strategytraining.com/mck-bcg-et-al-study-p9-ready-to-update-your-team-after-week-2

PAUSE & REFLECT

> Would the analyses for this engagement change substantially if we were advising a publicly listed bank?

> Would the analyses change for a bank owned by a PE firm, sovereign wealth fund, cooperative structure, or technology company?

WEEK 2 / PART 1: INTERVIEWS, STUDIES, MEETINGS

OTHER BOOKS
BY KRIS SAFAROVA:

...and more!
Available on Amazon.

OTHER BOOKS
BY KRIS SAFAROVA:

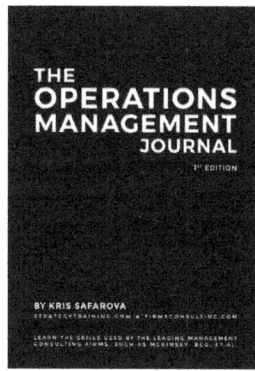
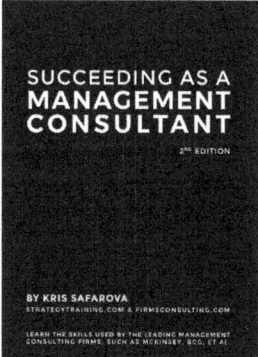
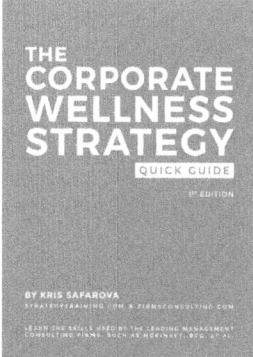
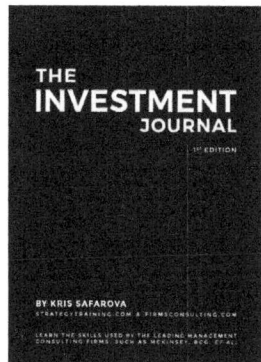

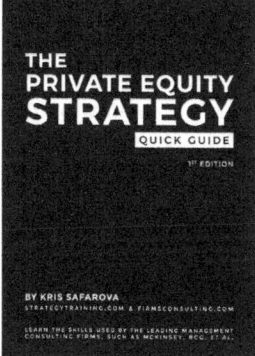

...and more!
Available on Amazon.

EXCLUSIVE STRATEGY, CONSULTING, PROBLEM-SOLVING, CRITICAL THINKING, LEADERSHIP, SALES, COMMUNICATION AND ENTREPRENEURSHIP SKILLS TRAINING.

All done by ex-McKinsey, BCG et al. partners.

STRATEGYTRAINING.COM

RESULTS OUR CLIENTS REPORT:
- being consistently promoted ahead of their peers
- being able to meaningfully enhance their firm's reputation and brand
- ability to grow their business/firm's revenue
- being positioned as a top performer in the mind of clients and leadership
- being viewed as a person on the team who must be placed on the most important projects
- being asked by clients that they should be on clients' engagements

To subscribe visit
FIRMSconsulting.com
and select annual premium membership.

EDITABLE ONLINE SLIDES WITH UNIQUE
METHODOLOGIES AND CONSISTENT DESIGN.

Full Studies

Proposals

Templates

THE ROI POTENTIAL

What is the value of securing seven-figure engagements?

What is the value of being promoted ahead of your peers?

What is the value of enhancing your firm's reputation and brand?

What is the value of growing your firm versus closing your firm?
What is the value of skyrocketing your career versus being counseled to leave as a weak performer?

What is the value of your superiors starting to see you as "the person" they need for the most important projects?

What is the value for clients to ask that you should be on their engagements?

To apply for SLIDES membership email
support@FIRMSconsulting.com

FIRMSCONSULTING

MASTERMIND & HIGH LEVEL PROGRAMS

In-depth systematic training series.

Weekly coaching and community mentorship.

Done For You templates and guides.

Consistent support and access to FIRMSconsulting's in-house team.

FOR MORE DETAILS, CONTACT
support@FIRMSconsulting.com

DUE TO PAGE NUMBER RESTRICTIONS FOR PRINT BOOKS, THIS BOOK IS SPLIT INTO 2 PARTS.

YOU CAN FOLLOW THE REST OF THE ENGAGEMENT IN PART 2.

Made in the USA
Middletown, DE
26 August 2022

72305326R00275